D0603357

0

REC'D

GIULIO CARLO ARGAN

THE BAROQUE AGE

CONTENTS

THE BAROQUE

The meaning of the word Baroque is still an open question. When Benedetto Croce wrote a great "History of the Baroque Age," he included in the term every manifestation of seventeenth-century life, morals, religion, politics, literature, figurative art; and his judgment of them all was unfavorable. The Baroque epoch, he said, in Italy at least, was one in which false values reigned: cerebral, moralizing, affected, and over-emphatic. For Eugenio D'Ors, however, the Baroque age was the expression of a category of the mind, of a vital Dionysian and irrational impulse. In spite of their contradiction, both of these views reveal that it is impossible to separate, at that period of history, the various forms of culture from the life which people then lived. Whether real or assumed, the irrational character of the age, which seems to have dominated the whole century, was due to the influence which all intellectual activities exerted on everyday life. There can be no doubt that the culture of the seventeenth century was irrational; but it was consciously irrational, always controlled and deliberate. It came neither from a profound vital impulse, as D'Ors contends, nor was it false and artificial, as Croce regards it. Today we know that the structure of modern society has its foundations in Baroque culture, which would hardly be the case if the Baroque age had been one of decadence, nor if it had been a return to the elemental vitality of primitive society. Clearly the men of this period turned from one kind of rationality, from "natural reason," and sought to work out another kind, an "artificial reason," as it might be called. Man's behavior was no longer motivated by natural forces or divine revelation, but by his peculiar situation as a social animal. We may describe this "artificial reason" which replaces "natural reason" as "social reason."

Although extended to all forms of life, the term Baroque applies above all to art, as a tangible manifestation of the movement, rhythm and values of life. The chief characteristic of seventeenth-century irrationalism was therefore a tendency to display itself or to exteriorize itself, minimizing the traditional prestige of abstract thought, and excluding all values which cannot be conveyed through the senses. Here art possesses a special importance, because it can translate everything into images which catch and delight the eye. It is therefore right to seek in art the most authentic and complete expression of a civilization which greatly enlarged the horizon of reality, setting scarcely any limits to the field of visual perception. This does not mean that all values and all activities had to be expressed through art. For the seventeenth century was, on the contrary, a century of specialization; every discipline, every human activity, had its own sphere of action and developed its own methods. Art too became specialized, and never aspired to be anything more than art. But now, considered in relation to the whole field of human endeavor, the function of art was to translate everything into images, and to exploit the concrete value of the image as a means of increasing man's awareness of the visible world. Science, religion, politics and daily life provided the "raw materials" of art. But as a means of deepening and enriching our sense of life, art became autonomous, and its task was to give expression to what was most vital and most characteristic in the culture of the time.

The word Baroque was applied to the art of the seventeenth century by the theorists and critics of the following century, the century of rationalism and, in art, of Neoclassicism. Because the Renaissance was an age in which "natural reason" triumphed, we may describe the Baroque as an irrational transition period between two rational periods. Here we may be over-simplifying, for there are deep differences between the rationalism of the Renaissance and that of the eighteenth century. The age of reason does not mark the beginning of a fresh inquiry; it did little more than try and put some order into the huge mass of contradictory experiences of the preceding century. The eighteenth century was an age of criticism, but the object of the criticism was the rich and disorderly fund of experience bequeathed by the seventeenth century. This is a further argument against the view that the Baroque period was one of decadence, or even of interruption. The seventeenth century was but the inevitable phase of transition during which one form of rationalism changed, to reappear in another form. It was then, for the first time, that men became aware of many of the problems which, in the centuries to come, developed into important issues.

The Renaissance believed that the world manifested in its completely logical structure the supreme rationalism of the Creator. By knowing nature man knew simultaneously God and himself, because man is made in the image of God; and the behavior of man, his moral conduct, depends on his knowledge of the eternal truth hidden beneath the changing and illusory appearances conveyed by his senses. Eighteenth-century thinkers, however, took a very different view. The age of reason no longer admitted any revealed or *a priori* truth. The world is, and cannot help being, the object of human thought; but since we know nothing of its real structure and form, all we can do is to examine and analyze the thought processes from which we derive our knowledge of the physical world, and to ensure that our thought follows a rational method. But how can this be done if there is no *a priori* rational principle? Because we cannot judge on premises, we judge on results. A good result, or only a useful one, is the fruit of right methods. Judgment is therefore the criticism of the means employed for obtaining a certain effect.

In the second half of the sixteenth century, the idea that human reason was created on the model of a divine logic, which expressed itself equally in created nature and in the dogmatic revelation of the scriptures, lost favor. This idea had stated that rational truth and revealed truth were identical in their essence, if not in their development. All phenomena had until now been part and parcel of a structure which identified them with a divine revelation. The disappearance of this structure gave back to the phenomena their multiplicity and their limitless diversity. Autonomy succeeds subordination, and the law which united all these autonomous facts is no longer considered as a divine law *a priori*, but the structure of the human spirit which perceives them and co-ordinates them. Every phenomenon is now

presented as a fact in itself, limited but endowed with a presence and an attraction which are quite new. They are no longer the different signs of a unique order, but a very varied whole, very much alive with materials for which the human spirit must now find a correlation, even if this is forced upon it by the social system. But this correlation is not necessarily logical or causal. We understand from it why the seventeenth-century artists showed such curiosity in the singularity and diversity of phenomena, but were so hesitant about their meaning. Each artist attempts to establish it personally, until perhaps he comes to realize that it does not exist absolutely, and that the recording of these phenomena by the human spirit is of value above all for establishing certain points of agreement which will permit men of the same time and place, taking part in the same historical situation, to understand one another, that is to say to communicate with one another.

At the origin of the radical transformation which the relations of man and the universe underwent in the seventeenth century, we must mention the religious crisis of the sixteenth century, no less important in this respect than the Cartesian revolution or, in the scientific domain, the appearance of Copernicus and Galileo. Without becoming involved in an examination of the doctrinal reasons which distinguish the two religious currents of the period, we can see that religious unity no longer existed, and that man found himself before an alternative, forced to choose not only between two theological doctrines but two codes of behavior. It was a question of a moral choice, and the natural order of creation, if one admits that one still believes in the existence of a system in nature, is of no help. All interest is now concentrated on the problem of human existence, its end and its destiny; for if salvation by grace is hazardous, salvation by works has no less its problems and its difficulties.

The phenomena which arise at the essence of these problems do not belong so much to nature as to man's life and, because such is his lot, to the conditions of his life in society. The phenomena of nature, numberless and of many kinds, are no more than the setting, the surroundings in which human existence takes place. The question of conduct then appears much more important than that of human nature, and as conduct only takes on its full meaning in the social sphere, everything bearing on society and its methods of organization becomes an essential pre-occupation. The schism which separated the Christian religion into two antagonistic groups, that of the Reformation and that of the Catholic Church, brings with it the idea of salvation or condemnation, both collective, dependent first on the choice that the individual makes. It also presents the problem of a faith and a social behavior. The Reformed Church limited individual autonomy by countermanding the principle of free choice, while the Catholic Church saw in the faith and a cult appealing to the masses the best method of avoiding heresy. In one case, as in the other, however, religion was more concerned with directing man's choice and behavior than in considering and describing the providential logic at the heart of the universe. The controversy caused the two camps to discover arguments suitable for directing this choice and for preventing defection. It is much more important under such conditions to persuade than to demonstrate.

In the absence of a single principle or model controlling all phenomena, we may conclude that the activities of the mind are also of various kinds. The field of demonstrable truth goes no further than the limits of science; morals are no longer founded on ontological truth. As for art, which reposes on the principle of imitation, we no longer know what it is supposed to imitate, although we may recognize that there are many ways of doing it. After a long journey together, science and art separate. For Piero della Francesca, science and art were one thing; for Leonardo, science and painting followed parallel and distinct roads. But between the science of Galileo and the art of his time, there was no longer any relation, and Galileo considered art in a critical way, from outside.

In fact, the more science declared that its aim (not its principle) was truth, the more art became aware that its only possible aim was fiction. But may one speak of fiction, and condemn it as morally negative, if there is no ascertainable truth? Is not scientific hypothesis a fiction until the moment when it is verified? May not fictive hypotheses exist which can be verified, not by demonstration of a logical kind, but by an image? Fiction has no doubt a certain value; but what value? Let us take an example. We all see that the sun turns around the earth, and that the sea is blue, and yet science tells us that it is the earth which turns around the sun, and that the water of the sea is colorless. But in our daily life we continue to measure time according to the movement of the sun from the east to the west; and when we see a blue stretch of water before us, we think of the sea. The appearance of things is responsible for these ideas, and we do not feel the need in our practical life to correct them according to the lessons of science. Existence is not entirely speculative, appearances have also their value; and we use them. We know that they are not exact representations of what happens in the universe, but we cannot deny that they too are phenomena, and phenomena which impinge on the human mind and have an influence on our behavior.

Previously, value was only attached to images which corresponded to unchanging forms of reality. Now all the images which crowded into the mind, whether transmitted by the senses from the exterior world or produced by the imagination, unquestionably possessed a real value. It even began to be doubted whether there are such things as images which contain an absolute content of truth. In the Renaissance, the pictures of a Bosch or a Bruegel seemed to be freaks of the imagination, dreams. In the seventeenth century, pictures which were equally remote from ordinary visual experience appeared perfectly plausible, or at least acceptable as more or less real creations of the imagination.

FORM AND IMAGE

The seventeenth century marks the beginning of an age which has been aptly described as the civilization of the image, and which is none other than our modern civilization. Between the Baroque and the Renaissance, which was the last civilization of form, lies Mannerism which is distinguished by a crisis of form. Neoclassicism, which followed the Baroque, tried to confer a rational order on the image, but the image was never again to find the logical structure or intellectual content of form as the representation of a positive conception of the world.

Baroque was a reaction against the distortion of form systematically practised by the Mannerists. Its intention, however, was not to restore the absolute and universal value of form, but to affirm openly the autonomous and intrinsic value of the image. To the theorists of the seventeenth century, it was clear that the "genius" peculiar to the artist is imagination, a faculty clearly distinct from the one which produces concepts and notions, and even from that combined activity of the intellect and the imagination which, during the Renaissance, produced with equal ease tangible forms and abstract concepts.

To understand the scope of this transformation we must go back to the end of the fifteenth century, when the Roman Church ended its schisms and placed its authority on the principle of historic antiquity, thereby identifying rational truth, historical truth, and dogmatic truth. This identity was understood and developed in different ways. In Florence, where the dominant culture was Neoplatonic, faith and intellect were identified in a common aspiration to transcend the experience of history and nature, and attain supreme truth in the Idea. In Padua, where the dominant culture was Aristotelian, the essential value was experience of nature and history, as a revelation in time of the divine logos. The rhythmic continuity of line and color in Botticelli, and the purity of the formal structure in Mantegna, clearly represent this polarity. The Florentine position allowed only one alternative: to carry the quest of the Idea to its logical conclusion, to the "sublime," turning its back on the experience of nature and of history (Michelangelo), or instead to renounce every *a priori* ideal, to refuse every principle of authority, to select the way of methodical doubt, of direct experience which is analytical and unprejudiced by phenomena (Leonardo). The Venetian attitude, in the case of Bellini and Giorgione, developed with a continually widening experience of nature and the human soul, in a "discourse" which was not always logical or historically justified, but was lively, full of emotion, intense, capable of expressing in all their subtlety the deepest levels of human feeling (Titian, Tintoretto, Veronese).

At the beginning of the sixteenth century Raphael attempted a synthesis of these different tendencies in a form which was unitary, syncretistic, universal. This man, whose art was purely classical, regarded nature and history, together, as expressions of divine providence, just as idea and experience are two ways, which are not contradictory, of recognizing the Creator in the creature and of making man's thought and action depend on the eternal logic of God. Dogma is a truth of faith, but founded on the logic of nature and history. It does not therefore limit "worldly" existence. In this way, Raphael did not hesitate to gather up in a form tending to the universal all the emotion of Venetian color. Dogma as a revelation contains all the forms of the tangible; but dogma without form would not be a revealed dogma, which would be absurd. The absolute and universal character of dogma makes it co-extensive with the whole gamut of tangible appearances. Art, which reveals the essential form of the world, is precisely the tangible and formal revelation of dogma. The Roman Church, in its role as the visible manifestation of God's presence on earth, needed art as spectacular evidence of its own rites, in order to make visible its own essence to the faithful, completely revealing it, and to demonstrate that nature and history, which are expressions of the will of God, reflect its logic. The artist is he who shows this formal logic to man and, because Divine Creation is a perfectly finished achievement, artistic form is a closed system of parts which are in equilibrium or exact relation. Bramante's project for the new Basilica of St Peter's, the temple symbolizing the union of all Christians, is a system of parts in perfect equilibrium; it is therefore a natural form which displays the equilibrium of the universe by its volumes where mass and space compensate one another, and at the same time a historical form, because it reunites and combines the two classical types of architecture, the Constantinian basilica and the Pantheon. But it is also a logical form, because its masses and its spaces have an almost syllogistic relation to one another, a relation of cause and effect.

Soon however the crisis of this syncretism of logic and faith appears. Already in the case of Leonardo nature does not have a logical form. It is without a constant structure; it is not a closed system nor, even less, a revealed truth. To know nature, it is necessary to study it closely and abandon all dogmatic prejudices. Knowledge of nature can be of value in worldly existence, but not for saving one's soul. For Giorgione nature is a factual reality, but full of hidden meanings. It can only be understood in one way—by becoming one with it, and feeling the mystery of the soul as an aspect of the mystery of nature. For Titian both history and nature present the same dramatic intensity of lively forces and contrasts. In his case emotion replies immediately to the sudden appearance of the phenomenon. Michelangelo prefers faith to experience, first abandoning the experience of nature, and then of history: the end is a direct and personal meeting with God (it was well known that he was in contact with the Roman circles of the "Catholic Reform" of Juan de Valdés), and this excludes the mediation of history and nature; art is no longer a mediating form of representation, but a means of ascetic exaltation. The impulse which forces man towards God however is still a will, a thirst for intellectual knowledge: he looks for God because his intellect desires truth, but the absolute truth of God is different from the relative truth of nature and history. To reach God logic is not enough, but love is required; and love, in its turn, is no more than a superior form of the intellect. But if God is the final goal, he is no longer the *a priori* form of creation, that is to say a form

which can change in its accidental and exterior appearance but remain unchanged in substance. God is an idea, an incorporeal image which is beyond matter and the physical world.

Mannerism was born with Michelangelo. From the outset it was an art which felt no need to imitate nature; or, more precisely, an art which set out to be a mimesis not of nature but of ideas. It may seem strange that the Mannerist crisis of form at the end of the sixteenth century was accompanied by extreme formalism. What happened was that form became hampered by "rules," and in this way lost its rational structure, its intellectual or learned content, its power of demonstration. Form ceased to be form because it refused totally to be a world form; it no longer *formed* experience and survived itself as a simple image. If form always reveals the presence of the real, which it professes to represent, the image, with its power of simple evocation, denotes its absence and retains only the fleeting shadow. Form renews itself continually, because it is born from an intuition or discovery of the real; the image is transmitted, and with it is transmitted the memory of ancient meanings, to which new ones are added. But, having no intellectual substance, it changes through an uninterrupted play of analogies, associations, combinations, contaminations, only bowing to occasional exigencies. A good example of this is the *contaminatio* of the classical divinities Hermes and Athena, described by Cartari as Hermathena, and represented by Zuccari at Caprarola as a synthesis combining the ideas of theory (Athena) and practice (Hermes). From this capacity for the combination and proliferation of images comes the extraordinary development in late Mannerism of sacred and profane iconography. In fact, the more an attempt is made to fix it in a constant type the more the image proves unstable, and changeable.

Mannerism, while declaring itself the faithful disciple of classicism, is not so in fact; for if form, which preserves intact the rational structure of nature under the changing appearances of the senses, remains classical, the image on the other hand is anti-classical, because it retains certain exterior likenesses while continually changing the content. Moreover, classical art itself, if it is viewed as an ensemble of abstract norms and no longer as a historical reality, is thereby placed automatically in an anti-classical perspective. It is then no longer a formal principle

ANNIBALE CARRACCI (1560-1609). DECORATIONS IN THE GALLERY OF THE FARNESE PALACE, ROME, 1597-1604.

PIETRO DA CORTONA (1596-1669). GLORIFICATION OF THE REIGN OF URBAN VIII, 1633-1639. BARBERINI PALACE, ROME.

universally applicable, but an immense repertoire of images with varied meanings and combinations, capable of multiplying almost spontaneously.

Tasso's influence was important in accelerating this crisis which renewed aesthetic values. Beauty no longer is a well-defined form with its contours, its proportions, its plastic shape, its colors, but the indefinite image which appears fleetingly in our imagination, generally when our imagination is confronted with a dramatic situation. Ariosto gave a precise description of form in the case of a beautiful woman: the face, the breasts, the arms, the legs, the proportions of the limbs, the color of the hair, the eyes, the cheeks. The figure which is described is fixed for us in a well-elaborated and unchangeable form. Tasso is content merely to say that the woman has "fine limbs," adding to the vague image of beauty which these words awake in the mind of the reader, one or two details connected with the situation where this beauty is revealed; the nobility of her walk, her proud look, her blushing or paleness through discontent, shame, anger. The well-built form of Ariosto permits the intervention of feeling in so far as it is only concerned with a feeling tied to nature; the sensitive rhythms of Tasso, charged with emotion, allow the image to express moral sentiments and their alteration according to different situations. Finally, the suppleness and the variability of the images give the artist complete licence to use them in the manner best suited to produce any desired effect or emotion. Form has reached the limits of its function when its construction has brought about an equilibrium, while the image is always connected with a goal which transcends it and is always subject to change.

CARRACCI   CORTONA   GAULLI

The crisis of the conception of nature as a revealed and eternal form of creation was reflected, at the beginning of the seventeenth century, in the two opposing styles of Caravaggio and Annibale Carracci. The breakdown of the old conception of nature led in the case of Caravaggio to a vivid and immediate rendering of reality; in the case of Annibale Carracci and his followers, it led to a quest for the origin and raison d'être *of art, in other words to a return to the past. The great age of Baroque decoration begins with Annibale's frescoes in the gallery of the Palazzo Farnese (1597-1604). These mythological scenes are what were called* quadri riportati; *that is to say, they were planned like easel pictures and transferred into a simulated architectural setting adorned with herms and caryatids. The forms are a conscious, nostalgic imitation of those of the classical tradition. There can no longer be any direct connection with nature; it can only be evoked through the images of a day long past when all human experience was experience of nature. These images come alive thanks to the artist's sense of history; but only imagination can carry us into a time remote from the present; and art born of the imagination is decorative because it is based on an ideal of beauty already fully achieved in the past, which it revives in the present. So that the more "imaginative" art is, the greater its concern to make the imaginary appear natural. Such is the case with Pietro da Cortona's* Glorification of the Reign of Urban VIII *(1633-1639), in which the device of the* quadro riportato *disappears and the whole composition is set in movement, the figures floating among simulated entablatures, caryatids, and clouds. The decoration is no longer a myth or fable, it is oratorical and theatrical; Cortona makes no attempt to conceal the artifice of it all, thus showing that for him painting is the appropriate medium for allegorical glorification. In his ceiling fresco in the church of the Gesù (1674-1679) Gaulli uses the abstract symbol of Christ's monogram as a source of physical light and extends the space of the church into the painted sky, which is filled with angels and saints. He is trying to show that this miraculous vision is the logical sequel of the continuous miracle of providence operating on earth through the medium of the Church. The figuration is now no longer either fictitious or oratorical; it is a hymn of praise.*

GIOVANNI BATTISTA GAULLI, CALLED BACICCIA (1639-1709). THE TRIUMPH OF THE NAME OF JESUS, 1674-1679. CHIESA DEL GESÙ, ROME.

THE FUNCTION OF IMAGES

The religious crisis of the sixteenth century directly affected art as a tangible form of dogma and as a necessary means of church ritual. This visible manifestation of the truth of faith was the scandal which the Reformation condemned as a survival of paganism. This tangible, even sensual, mediation between humanity and God cannot be admitted, now that every form of spiritual mediation has been put aside, and men are even suspicious of the scriptures. Every intermediary between man and God, whether it be nature, history, the Church, or art, is by definition an illusion and a sin. Not even the theorists of the Counter-Reformation dared to defend the use of images *in toto*; they recognized that the accusation of paganism against the art of the Renaissance was not entirely baseless, and they protested against the profane images which filled the churches. They distinguished however between good and bad images. The image in itself is neither bad nor good, but it can be used for a good or a perverted end. It is not a question of the true and the untrue, but of the useful and the harmful. It is not possible to formulate a theory of images as a theory of forms can be formulated, but it is possible to use images in a political sense, and this is what at the end of the sixteenth century was done by Gilio in his "Two Dialogues... of the Errors of Painters concerning Histories" (1564), by Ammannati (1582), Paleotti (1582) and, at the beginning of the seventeenth century, Federico Borromeo (1625).

The defense and revaluation of images was the great undertaking of the Baroque age; it started when the Church, now convinced that it had contained the Protestant attack, passed to the counter-offensive. In the face of the iconoclast Reformation, the Roman Catholic Church reaffirmed the ideal value and practical necessity of visible demonstrations, as an edifying example, from the events of her own history. The Church reaffirmed again the validity of classical culture and of that of the Renaissance because, if what is beautiful gives pleasure, it can serve as a means of persuasion. It encouraged the most spectacular forms of art, just as it accentuated the spectacular character of religious worship and ritual. But at the moment of its greatest danger, the Church fundamentally re-examined its own program and aims. The doctrine of the rational form of the universe, revealed in the scriptures and developed by the scholastic philosophers and theologians, was breaking down. The Church could no longer continue to deny, relying upon the specious interpretation of sacred texts, the evidence of geographical discoveries, or of the new physical science; nor could art, if it was to be of service to the Church, continue to represent as fixed and constant a reality which science described as in continuous movement and change. But the notion that Baroque art with its ever moving forms was intended to represent the universe in its constant state of flux does not bear examination. The structure of the universe, whether fixed or mobile, no longer interests the artist, just as it no longer continued, except in very restricted terms, to furnish matter for dogma or arguments of a doctrinal nature. Another difficulty attributable to the changing times: having already decided not to evaluate images according to ontological truths, the Church found herself confronted by the moral problem bound up with that faculty of the human mind which produces images (i.e. the imagination) and which had necessarily to be submitted to the criteria of the good or the bad, of the useful or the harmful, like all human actions. The activity of the imagination may operate according to divine design, and then it will lead to good, or it can be inspired by the Devil, and then it will lead to bad. When heresy is threatening on all fronts, sins of thought are no less grave than bad actions. If it leads to good, the function of images is practical, educative, and didactic; but this function cannot be performed merely by transmitting moral exhortations and edifying examples with the aid of images. The Church wished to display in art the origin and universal extension of her own authority; this forced her, rather than to spread the truth of faith, to influence human behavior and all the actions of men regardless of their social rank or cultural level. Nor is this valid only for religious authority, but for authority in general, starting with that of the state, which descends from religious authority and also aims at co-ordinating the conduct of men towards a certain goal, but it operates in a different domain which is much more worldly. The state in an absolute monarchy certainly preserves the different levels of social hierarchy, but it places all individuals in the same situation of subjection vis-à-vis the sovereign. A society which desires henceforth to be a reality of the first order and a unitary organism, will stress these specific differences in its body which characterize the being and behavior of different classes and individuals. These different ways of being, and this variety of class interests, must therefore be taken into consideration, if the movement is to be towards a common goal, which for the Church is salvation, and for the State power.

The image has no influence on our actions or decisions; its effect is on intentions. It does not provide a plan of action, it is only an appeal. This clearly will be the more effective according as it is more suited to the attitudes, interests and customs of the various social classes. A hierarchical structure still plays a role in the transmission of these appeals, and it does so from the top to the bottom. But there is a tendency now in the social pyramid for the movement to be from the bottom to the top, and to permit increasingly the inferior classes to take part in matters of general interest. It was not only as a result of a kind of aping curiosity that, in the seventeenth century, art was concerned with documenting in images the manner of life of the bourgeois and proletarian classes; and it was not for ideological reasons that this documentation was infinitely more lively and animated than that of the official portraits, not to speak of religious iconography, whether historical or devotional. The true protagonist in these scenes of social customs was not the proletariat or the bourgeoisie, as a particular social class, but the historical personage whom Guicciardini had called "the private man," the man who was not seeking a universal view of things, but who wanted a clear objective idea of reality. For the purposes of practical existence or utility, communication at the level of the image appears more effective than that at the intellectual level of form and conception,

because it means simply "taking note" without any speculative effort, and does not turn the spirit away from the immediate and practical exigencies of life.

In the politico-social program of the Church, then, art became an essential instrument for the new kind of religious life which St Francis of Sales, in the first years of the century, described and explained to Christians as "devotion." It was the means of reaching salvation through works, that is by living in the world and carrying out social duties: "The act of devotion should be practised in a different manner among gentlemen, artisans, servants, princes, widows, unmarried women, and married women; in addition the practice of devotion should be adapted to the strength, the duties, the tasks of each particular person." Devotion may then be described as reducing religious life to *praxis*; the devout person does not demand the demonstration of supreme truth, but he selects a certain manner of behavior.

The demonstration of a truth is identical for everyone, while the ways of being are numerous, although a single goal directs them all. The Church we see therefore has many problems. Among others is that of the pagan peoples who have entered and become part of the human community, and who must be initiated into Christian life. If such a large part of humanity is not yet Christian, and must therefore await the revelation, we may conclude that the revelation has not been completed. But as this thesis would give ammunition to the Protestants, the Catholic Church affirmed that the revelation is complete, but that it is the responsibility of Christians to carry it to those who do not possess it. This missionary task, consisting, on the one hand, of the defense of the faithful from the danger of heresy and, on the other, of extending the Catholic community to peoples in recently discovered continents, is effected by "propaganda." Propaganda does not demonstrate, it persuades; and it persuades people to be devout. There are various levels of propaganda; classical culture, for example, can act when it is addressed to men sensitive to the bond which providentially unites modern and ancient history, and moral life with intellectual life. But the ignorant, pagans, primitive peoples, if they cannot understand the classical language of form, are sensitive to the message of the images. Thus a new and ample iconography of Christ was born, of the Madonna, of the saints (we should not forget that here we are addressing peoples who were originally polytheist and idolators) and a new, simple, direct type of symbol (for example the Heart of Jesus). Devotional images do not exalt the "historical" figure, and they tend towards realism, or rather towards a kind of naturalism. Their aim is to show that heroic virtue is not exclusively the property of the ancients and of great men; but that anyone can become a saint, even if he lives in human society, and carries out his own social duties with a devout mind. For this new kind of election, the images offer a new road or, as Francis of Sales said, a ladder. The prose itself of his "Introduction to the Devout Life" is an example of the "devotional" style, clear, precise, descriptive, full of images which are clearly "functional" because they are directly explicit.

"Differentiated" devotion is, in reality, none other than politics. In fact, if the end is the salvation of the human species, the politics of the state, as a collective body, must be a means and an instrument of salvation. The Protestants too (it is sufficient to think of Calvin) accept the transformation of religion into politics, and the principle *cuius regio eius religio,*" sanctified with the Peace of Augsburg (1555), made possible an identification between the confessional and the national struggles, and set the stage for what was to be the dramatic history of the seventeeth century. Henceforth politics no longer depended upon the decisions of the "great ones"; they concerned everyone. The ever-growing network of traffic, which was becoming intercontinental, the accumulation of riches by the mercantile bourgeoisie, the great financial loans required by the new methods of warfare, their economic consequences, the decline of the old feudal system and the rise of capitalism, enormously extended the field in which the determining forces of political life were born and acted. The rulers themselves tended moreover to remove power from the feudal aristocracy, seeking their support on a wider base, in the bourgeoisie which held the economic power, and in the people who were becoming conscious of their own strength. Since the choice of religion (and this was already appearing as an ideological choice) can determine the movement of masses, and compromise the equilibrium of the political forces, ideological persuasion (religious or political) becomes the essential manner for the exercise of authority: its instrument is still propaganda, and propaganda operates on the level of, and by means of, images. There is an indirect propaganda which prepares the spirit of man in a general way for the tasks which will from time to time be demanded; there is a direct propaganda, which aims at an immediate and determined goal. All, or nearly all, the art of the seventeenth century was animated, on various levels and in various directions, by a spirit of propaganda, at least in the sense that its images act as images, and not for eventual implicit conceptions. It is true that the seventeenth century is the century of the great allegories, but the allegories are not images reduced to concepts; on the contrary, they are concepts reduced to images. There is no attempt to make the image a concept, but rather to give to the concept, transposed into image, a force which does not support a demonstration but, as in the quality of the image, a practical entreaty. Even the movements of artistic currents and tastes develop by a mechanism which could be called propaganda. In the sixteenth century, the diffusion of classicism throughout Europe was achieved as a result of analyses, of judgment, and finally of the acceptance of certain facts and certain values whose ensemble formed one culture. In the seventeenth century, cultural relations in the visual arts were propagated, almost as an epidemic, by certain types of images, and often through the intellectually null but psychologically powerful factor of fashion. The very fact that the declared aim of Baroque poetics was the "marvelous," which implies the suspension of the intellectual faculty, demonstrates in what zones of the human mind propaganda was to act through the image—on the imagination in fact, considered as the source and the impulse of feelings, which in their turn were to be forced into action.

The art of the seventeenth century has been accused of being oratorical, of exalting the "great men" and the divine springs of authority; although, as Croce has observed, this mania for greatness had its counterpart in the taste for minute description, full of detail, sometimes pedantic. Often there is a distinction between court art, with its "grand manner," and bourgeois art, with its modest and descriptive manner, identifying the first with a so-called Italian and French Baroque classicism, the second with Flemish and Dutch art. The distinction is not entirely justified. Both Italy and France produced at the time quite as many examples of genre painting as Flanders and Holland did of history painting (it is enough to cite the names of Rubens and Rembrandt); and it is by no means rare to see the same artists practising both types of work, which clearly belong, by analogy or contradiction, to the same cultural orbit.

To explain the apparent contradiction, we must remember the new position of the artist in society. His prestige was undoubtedly less than it had been in the preceding century, when he was patronized by Popes, princes, and noblemen, on familiar terms. But his professional autonomy was now much greater. Henceforth, he is the middle-class professional man, like the doctor or the lawyer; as such he disposes of a specific technique, and this technique is also a culture, because it bears not only on the material execution of his works, but also on the formulation and elaboration of his images. In fact, he is asked to take part in all things which require any use of images (public spectacles, funerals, ceremonies, etc.). The princes and kings are only the great clients of the artist; beside them there is another clientele, the rich bourgeoisie, and by means of prints the work of art also reached the lower classes. The system of direct commissioning of a work of art declined; between the artist and the public, from now on, stood the dealer. Artists, or at least painters, began working without commission, producing works destined for anyone who could pay for them. Genre painting deals with human figures painted not to please one man, but a class. Artists catered henceforth for a public which was influenced by their work, but a public whose own aspirations, opinions and demands in turn exerted an influence on the work of art. With this rose a system of criticism which became a lively part of artistic life. As art was now supposed to exercise a social function, it was necessary to explain the intentions and methods of the artist. Art had become a technique of persuasion, and persuasion presupposes an open bilateral relationship; if it operated in only one direction, from high to low, it would be under constraint and therefore, to make itself understood, would not require the suggestive power of images. If it is to persuade, it must answer to the desire of being persuaded. Art has now become no longer the creation of persons endowed with a strong imagination; it develops and educates the imagination, which becomes in this way an essential function of the mind. Moreover, there cannot be any social and political interest without a social and political imagination, without a certain ability to foresee

events ahead which, although they have indispensable premises in the past, can no longer be conceived as simple effects of certain causes.

Social and political imagination is a new fact, and it is the counterpart of the practical spirit of the bourgeoisie, of its positive conception of existence. From the fact that artists were no longer courtiers but middle-class professionals, it might be inferred that the traditional distinction between a court art bound up with power and an art of the middle classes was more apparent than real. Actually the so-called court art was not so much an instrument of authority as an image which the bourgeoisie gave itself of authority. Otherwise, why should authority have had recourse to persuasion rather than to constraint? It is clear, on the other hand, that the manner of representing authority, generally allegorically, is not intended to make it seem present and in action before the eyes of the spectator; on the contrary, it makes it less concrete, transfers it from the realm of facts to that of ideas, and reduces it to a formal rather than a material reality. From the moment that authority selected persuasion, it destroyed itself. If Rubens embodied great ideas in beautiful opulent women, it was because he instinctively saw that an appeal to the senses would be more effective than a demonstration of abstract ideas.

As a bourgeois professional, the artist is a technician, and the new class was keenly interested in all the possibilities of technique. We should not forget that the first act of the bourgeoisie was the transformation of technique, the organization of artisan production, and the creation of an industrial system. The so-called "excesses" of Baroque art may certainly appear incongruous in terms of the practical spirit of the bourgeoisie. They will not appear so, however, if one reflects that these "excesses" had a purely instrumental reason; they were expedients devised to attain a specific end, their purpose being to arouse a sense of wonder, that is a break with every habit, and a projection of thought by means of the imagination into the domain of the possible. Art demonstrates that even the images which are most remote from common experience can, as a result of technique, be made perceptible, credible, and communicable. Imagination, in fact, has a function not unlike that of the hypothesis in science, and in the same way it is more valid for its productivity than for its possible content of truth.

CARRACCI   RENI

Hercules at the Crossroads, *painted by Annibale Carracci between 1595 and 1597 for the "Camerino" of the Palazzo Farnese in Rome, is a classical "fable" like the mythological scenes in the gallery of the same palace. But the mythological theme in this case implies a moral allegory: Hercules is confronted with the choice between vice and virtue, pleasure and duty, the transitoriness of worldly joys and the perpetuity of fame and history. The painting is a typical* montage *of elements with moral allusions. In the landscape background we see a rocky eminence with the steep path of virtue winding up to it, and a shady wood, which is an invitation to rest and pleasure; the figure of Virtue is a statue, that of Pleasure a dancer clad in transparent veils blown by the breeze. This allegorical landscape is nevertheless "naturalistic"—not in the sense that it is observed and taken from actual scenery, but in the sense that the abstract concepts find a "natural" expression in the forms of nature. As the ancients taught, the forms of nature are full of meaning, containing all the knowledge that is useful to man; and beauty, as ideal nature, is its tangible revelation.*

In the Massacre of the Innocents *(c. 1611), Guido Reni, who had just returned to Bologna from Rome and was still under the influence of Caravaggesque "realism," represents the historical event as an action having no development in space and time. In keeping with Aristotle's* Poetics, *however, he gives the scene strict unity of time and place; he confines the strenuous movements of the figures within a clear geometrical structure, attempts to convey a visual expression of the two tragic emotions postulated by Aristotle (pity and terror), and embodies the idea of catharsis in the two angels descending from heaven with the palm of martyrdom. The background is not composed of landscape, but of architecture. For the transition from the harsh reality of the event to the spirituality of the idea does not require the mediation of nature: the severe classicism of the forms is enough to reveal the lofty religious and moral import of a scene so brutally tragic as this massacre of innocent children.*

ANNIBALE CARRACCI (1560-1609). HERCULES AT THE CROSSROADS, 1595-1597. MUSEO NAZIONALE DI CAPODIMONTE, NAPLES.

GUIDO RENI (1575-1642). THE MASSACRE OF THE INNOCENTS, ABOUT 1611. PINACOTECA, BOLOGNA.

PETER PAUL RUBENS (1577-1640). HENRY IV PRESENTED WITH THE PORTRAIT OF MARIE DE' MEDICI, ABOUT 1622. LOUVRE, PARIS.

When he painted Henry IV presented with the Portrait of Marie de' Medici *(c. 1622), Rubens transposed a recent event into an allegory. Henry IV had just become undisputed master of France, and he now decided to take a new wife, an event which coincided with the return of peace. A number of themes contribute to the allegory. The king is still armed, and in the distance the fires of war are still burning; but while Minerva urges him to prudence, two cupids play with his helmet and shield, which are now unwanted. Above, in the clouds, the forthcoming royal marriage is symbolized by that of Jupiter and Juno. As was customary at the time, the king was presented with a portrait of his bride, and it was this ceremony of presentation, which actually took place at court, that provided Rubens with the point of departure for this elaborate allegory. Thus we see an actual half-length portrait of the queen, duly framed, a picture within the picture, and a transparent allusion to the power of painting to kindle the emotions.*

Domenichino's treatment of historical and religious subjects is different from that of both Caravaggio and Reni. History painting, to his thinking, has no need of catharsis; it is itself a kind of catharsis inasmuch as events are ennobled by the manner and style of the narration. In his picture of St Cecilia distributing Clothes to the Poor *(1614-1615) he does not shrink from including plebeian motifs: children quarreling with each other, boys climbing on each other's shoulders to reach the terrace on which the saint is standing. But even these motifs are treated in a noble, classical, Raphaelesque manner. That the composition has been carefully worked out is shown by the deliberate repetition of verticals and horizontals, and the calculated distribution of figures, vertically, horizontally, and in depth. The lighting does not produce strongly contrasted shadows, and the light colors are well harmonized. It is a typically devout composition, particularly in the noble bearing with which the poor, the elect of God, are represented. The painting is, in fact, an invitation to take part in works of charity, and the tone throughout is simple, tranquil, and persuasive, as in a moral exhortation. In this devotional picture Domenichino echoes the literary style of St Francis of Sales.*

DOMENICHINO (1581-1641). ST CECILIA DISTRIBUTING CLOTHES TO THE POOR, 1614-1615. SAN LUIGI DEI FRANCESI, ROME.

POETICS AND RHETORIC

In the domain of ideas the Baroque undoubtedly represents a reaction against the philosophy of the Idea and mannerist Neoplatonism, and a return to the philosophy of experience. The two great sources of Baroque aesthetic thought are the *Poetics* and the *Rhetoric* of Aristotle, and their Latin derivatives.

Closely associated with the *Poetics* is the notion that the character of "mimesis" is more ethical than intellectual. Mimesis does not prescribe what to do, because it is possible to imitate different things in different ways; moreover, it can be the imitation of the better, the similar, or the worse. If tragedy is "mimesis of a serious action, which is completed in itself, with a certain extension in ornamental language... with instances which excite pity and terror, and its effect is to raise and glorify the spirit of these passions" (*Poetics*, iv.)—if this is so, it is clear that the definition applies perfectly well to the "type" of historical-religious Baroque composition, just as "ugliness without pain," indeed with the pleasure that imitation is always capable of producing, is simultaneously the fundamental motif of comedy and of genre scenes. There are, as we shall see, works which aim at recording in figurative art patterns which are complete equivalents of those of the tragedy and comedy of Aristotle.

The principle *"ut pictura poesis,"* a fundamental one for Baroque aesthetics, carries with it the essential question of verisimilitude and embraces the whole problem of the production of images, and of the difference between images which are useful and harmful. But it is important to observe that this distinction is no longer a matter of deciding whether or not the images conform to certain moral precepts; it is based, rather, on the whole process and mechanism of their production. Images produced through the process of verisimilitude are useful, while those produced through the arbitrary caprice of fantasy are harmful. It is not so much what one imagines which is important, but the way one imagines it; in fact, imagination has now become a concrete activity of the mind, a means of thinking through images rather than through logic. Aristotle stated that the domain of the possible is open to the poet, and that it is this which distinguishes him from the historian, who must deal with what has happened; but he adds that what is credible or possible is only that which has already happened (*Poetics*, ix. 9). For this reason, the serious imagination has a basis in the memory, and its premise is historical experience; it is this which prevents the imagination from wandering aimlessly in the undefined domain of chance. But the pure and simple repetition of an event can be achieved by chance, which would appear to contradict what we have just said. When however repetition is not due to chance, but to the laws of verisimilitude and necessity, the cardinal laws of history, then we are no longer dealing with a particular case but with a universal fact. Nor are we dealing with laws which can be reduced to logical causality; if everything were a logical relation of cause and effect, everything could be foreseen, and no foreseen fact would be able to excite pity or terror. A relation must exist between facts, but not such as will permit us to know beforehand what will happen after; coherence and foresight belong only to the plan conceived in the mind of the artist, and the end he achieves will be a surprise to the spectator. This occurs in many Baroque works of art, even in the absence of any explicit time sequence; an almost realistic representation of certain parts is accompanied by a miraculous vision, without the passage from one to the other appearing either obvious or absurd to the spectator. For example, a brutal depiction of the martyrdom of a saint, with its catharsis value, may be combined with a heavenly vision of the angels and saints in glory. An even closer relation can be discerned between the distribution of the various parts of tragedy (prologue, episode, exodium) and the compositional arrangement of Baroque paintings with historical and religious subjects: big figures in the foreground to introduce the action, then the episode, and finally echoes of the action fading into the distance in the background.

Aristotle's *Rhetoric* is a treatise on the art of persuading, by speech; but as Aristotle specifies, it is the speech in the Areopagus, the political speech. The application of the theory of the political speech to art is a new one, but the idea of art as *elocutio* comes from sixteenth-century Venice. Pino and Dolce praise the painting of Giorgione and of Titian, because the rigorous logic of the demonstrative argument of Mantegna has been dissolved in human speech, and all the inflections and subtleties of feeling have passed into art. In Tintoretto speech becomes excitable, pathetic, dramatic; he was the first artist to observe the suggestive force of Tasso's poetics, and the new value which the image takes on when, emptied of all plastic consistency, it gathers to itself a wealth of accents, subtleties and allusion. Beauty itself becomes the expression of a state of mind, or of a moral condition, which can be understood intuitively through a current of human sympathy. The first quality of the artist, then, becomes spontaneity, the natural fluidity of the speech; but this implies the complete mastery of expressive means, of technique. "*Ars est celare artem*," said Aristotle, meaning that the less you say you intend to persuade, the more you are able to persuade (*Rhetoric*, iii. 2).

Rhetoric does not deal with any specific material; it is a way of discovering, ordering and expounding "matters which are likely to persuade in any given subject" in a civilization in which "speech is the peculiar quality of man"; and not only speech but dialogue, even if one of the parties is confined to a listening role. For the orator behaves as if his interlocutor replied to him, interrupted him, questioned him, and made objections. But even if his aim is not to demonstrate the truth, it is not a mere verbal artifice: it takes into account the manners, the principles and values which, while not being absolute truths, have a foundation in the common conscience and tend to determine behavior. "The most important manner of persuading and giving good counsel is to be informed of all the fortunes of the state, to have a clear knowledge of its practices, laws, and those things which are of particular importance to each state, because everyone can be persuaded by what is useful. And what is useful to every state is what tends towards its conservation" (*Rhetoric*, i. 8).

The domain in which rhetoric is shown to its best advantage is the "polis," the city with its assemblies, its powers of deliberation and judgment. The character, temperament, passions, virtues and vices of individuals are certainly not suppressed in the state; but all these facts are no longer considered in relation to human nature, but rather to society. In the same way, Baroque art is addressed no longer to man as "the center of the universe," or in his relation to nature, but to man as he lives in a society, in which his situation is always different, because society has no definite or immutable form. Man is part of a certain tradition, of social customs; he has his prejudices and attitudes; he shares common ideas of what is good and what is not good, what is useful and what is not useful; his desires may be urgent or not pressing, precise or vague; his interests change according to circumstances; his conception of space and time is determined much more by his own situation in the world than by his ideas of the structure of the universe.

Aristotle says there are three kinds of rhetoric: the deliberative, the judicial and the demonstrative. "The time proper to each of these is as follows. For the deliberative orator it is the future, for in exhorting or dissuading he advises respecting things still to come. The time proper to a judicial pleader is the past, for it is always on the subject of actions already done that the one party accuses and the other defends. The demonstrative orator is concerned chiefly with the present, for it is in reference to things as they are that everyone either praises or blames. Nevertheless, orators often avail themselves of other times, as well by awakening a recollection of what has already happened as by anticipating what is likely to happen" (*Rhetoric*, i. 3). The kind of rhetoric whose expression is found in the art of the seventeenth century is the demonstrative, which regards the present as a meeting point between the experience of the past and the prospect of the future. Here we have a new conception of time; man lives in the present, but his decisions imply a reflection on his past, and a forward view to his future. History is no longer only a form of education and an example, but one of the data of the problem: the life of the individual and that of the community develop in a continuous sequence of premises and consequences, which are no longer reducible to the logic of cause and effect, because the problem of morals is more important than that of knowledge.

The historico-religious paintings of the seventeenth century incorporate this new idea of time in the composition and the very structure of the picture space. We pass from distant historical allusions to visions of celestial glory, from the bald delineation of an action to the vague promise of a future beatitude. There is almost always a direct reference to present experience: among persons wearing antique costume are others clad in modern clothes, with some detail in the painting so full of truth that the viewer feels that he can almost touch it—a basket of fruit, a bouquet of flowers, animals, and other objects which are painted with lively realism, but placed in an "imaginary" context.

There may be different kinds of rhetorical or persuasive speech; one may present without comment the irrefutable proof of facts. If the proof is not immediately clear and evident, it must be accompanied by arguments or enthymemes; if there is no proof, it must be replaced with argument. The "fact" can be considered as an event which happens under our eyes, a proof which has no need of comment (Caravaggio); or as a past experience which must be introduced again in the present, and presented as the present (Carracci); or it may remain fairly distant, no more than a recall, or an example in a speech interwoven with arguments and pleading (Pietro da Cortona). If we are to persuade effectively, we must first be convinced ourselves—not only of the truth or excellence of what we affirm and enjoin upon others, but even more of the possibility and the utility of human communication. Artists of the seventeenth century took pride in the technique of communication at their disposal, and often varied their techniques in accordance with the various ends they had in view. The principles of authority and the values proclaimed and extolled in their work are only the content, sometimes merely incidental, of their communication. The important thing is that communication should take place, and take place on all levels, by the most effective ways and means, direct and indirect.

The important thing is, in other words, that human communication should be open and total, inspired only by the keen desire of persuading everyone that certain things are useful or necessary, others harmful and to be avoided; that is, it must be inspired by the desire to form groups of loyal men with the same beliefs and opinions, beyond the preconceived limits of formal logic.

THE STATE
AND THE CAPITAL CITY

The great political creation of the seventeenth century was the nation-state, embodied in its most typical form, the absolute monarchy. Modern Europe was born in the seventeenth century as a system of states always tending towards a balance of power, a political and economic equilibrium. The Renaissance had produced an urban civilization in which the free communes had been replaced by cities claiming to be small sovereign states. They were not only the seat of their prince and the instrument of his personal policy, but heirs to a historical tradition, and centers of culture.

In the seventeenth century, the concentration of power in one city established its supremacy; it became the seat of authority, with the organs of government and public administration, and was the residence of foreign diplomatic representatives, while the remaining towns were reduced to the rank of regional administrative centers. There was now a "capital city" art and culture, sensitive to international currents and exchanges; and a "provincial city" art and culture which, although sometimes of a high order, suffered from the disadvantage of the town's peripheral position, and its remoteness from the broader currents of international thought.

With its new role as representative of the country, the capital tended to lose the traditional municipal character which had stamped it socially and architecturally. As a result of its position, generally in the center of the state, and the more modern methods of warfare, its defense against aggressors now took place far from the city walls; there was no need for walls, and it became less a fortified place than a center of roads and communications. The interior growth of the city, too, no longer depended on the initiative of its burgesses and municipality, but on its political rulers. Its physical appearance, which had been a reflection of the way of life of the whole urban community, now symbolized the intentions and aspirations to pomp and power of its rulers.

In layout, the capital city differed greatly from the medieval city with its division into districts. In future planning it had to envisage a rapid increase of population, an extensive traffic system, a political and administrative center, and, of course, provision for strong contingents of troops. Wheeled traffic demanded long, broad streets, converging in open squares, and the planning of the city increasingly depended on the layout of the streets. The city became a network of roads and communications; and the buildings which represented political and religious authority became the center of public life. The old relationship between city and countryside was also changed, and the classical antithesis between civilization and nature was replaced by a social distinction, that between town-dweller and peasant. If the capital city was conscious and proud of its history and past, it also looked confidently to the future; and plans for its growth were drawn up under the personal guidance of the sovereign or ruler.

The prototype of the capital city which also incorporated the ideas of the past was, and could only be, Rome. This was the first European city which the planners attempted to invest with the structure and appearance of a capital. But its glorious past, the ruins of the ancient city, were buried under a heterogeneous mass of dwellings, with here and there, emerging in isolated splendor, some patrician *palazzo* or stately church. In the middle of the fifteenth century, Pope Nicholas V decided that the Vatican deserved more dignified surroundings than these abandoned ruins. Once the schisms were ended, and the historical supremacy of the Church of Rome reaffirmed, the ruins could be regarded as symbols of the heroic past of the primitive Church. Leon Battista Alberti's plans for the reconstruction were based on the restoration of the ancient city; and his treatise on architecture, written in Rome in the middle of the century, was probably regarded as a guide for the "humanist" reconstruction of Rome. The report made to Leo X was conceived on these lines (formerly attributed to Raphael, but now, following Förster, to Bramante). The problem arose anew after the sack of Rome in 1527; and the new streets laid out in the second half of the sixteenth century destroyed the concentration of dwellings clustering around the Ponte Sant'Angelo. The only real urban reform was undertaken in the last years of the sixteenth century by Sixtus V, whose technical planner was Domenico Fontana. Now that the most dangerous phase of the Reformation, its open revolt, had been crushed, the Popes felt that, in a Europe evolving into a system of national states, the spiritual and supernational power of the Church could not be effective without the support of a temporal state. The capital of this state which was equally weak, both economically and militarily, was Rome. The new policy of equilibrium between states, which the Church now recognized formally, was based upon Rome's historical and moral prestige. For Rome was the goal of pilgrims from all the Catholic countries, and its "central position" had a political as well as a religious significance.

The purely physical aspect of the capital of the Catholic world was a powerful form of political and religious propaganda, and the *forma urbis*, as envisaged by Sixtus V and Domenico Fontana, became an important "rhetorical" means of persuasion. Because the new streets connected the ancient Christian basilicas, they had a devotional function. Pilgrims were attracted to the ancient basilicas, and the whole area was consecrated anew, and invested with an ideological quality. Just as production is the principal aim in an industrial city today, so in a "holy" city religion is all important. The city no longer belongs exclusively to its citizens; it is a Mecca for all foreigners, whom it must impress by the grandeur of its monuments; and its buildings must be so placed that they are easily accessible from the main roads leading to the city.

The Church did not succeed entirely in its aim of balancing the political forces of Europe, and the urban development of the capital came almost to a standstill after the death of Sixtus V, and the dismissal of Domenico Fontana. But the ideal conception of the capital city—as a visible expression of superior and transcendent authority—now existed, and the other European capitals aspired to it, if only theoretically. The clearest example of this

transformation of ancient cities into modern capitals was to be seen in Paris and London. The urban reforms of Paris were initiated by Henry IV, and continued under Louis XIV, from the plans of Blondel and Bullet; and under Louis XV, from those of Patte. The reconstruction of London after the Great Fire of 1666 was based on the designs of Christopher Wren (although few of them were put into effect). Madrid, too, underwent complete transformation in the seventeenth century. In Italy, Turin, the capital of the small but modern state of Piedmont, became a model for the structure of a capital city. In its checkerboard plan, with big regular squares, Turin kept to the plan of the original Roman *castrum*; this we may call its "humanist" side. But that plan also lent itself to military and civil parades, which display and emphasize the authority of the state, just as religious ceremonies display and emphasize the authority of the Church; this we may call its Baroque side.

The capital city, in its typically Baroque form, is a monument to what Lewis Mumford calls "the ideology of power." At least two new architectonic forms were established; the street and the square. Here too the models were Roman—the long Via delle Quattro Fontane designed by Fontana, and the portico of St Peter's by Bernini. They are open spaces, with perspectives, architectonically defined by the façade of the lateral buidings. The façades are no longer simply the front sides of closed volumes (i.e. of buildings), but they define the limits of empty open spaces, and are related to the street façade. The façade is no longer regarded in terms of the building to which it belongs; it becomes a surface area which can be extended indefinitely, and where architectonic form is defined by the rhythmic succession of the windows (there are many cases of this prolongation of old façades: the Palazzo Falconieri in Rome, for example, where the façade was almost doubled by Borromini). The urban layout now tends to be uniform and regular; but the monuments still remain, to emphasize the necessary elements of "decoration."

The great example of the city as an expression of the "ideology of power" was Paris, capital of the most powerful European monarchy, and center of a state whose authority had arrogated to itself Divine Right (while at the same time carrying out a most realistic form of power politics). In the second half of the seventeenth century, Christopher Wren, the great architect of the reconstruction of London, declared that "Paris is probably the finest school of architecture in Europe." He confirmed these words on his travels, for he never went to any other city to study. Yet Pevsner says, "At the time of Inigo Jones's *Wanderjahre*, Paris was no more than a stopping-place on the road to Rome." It is clear that Wren, with his remarkable flair, was referring here less to great monumental architecture, which continued in Rome to produce exemplary works, than to civic architecture, above all to private architecture, with its utilitarian and decorative sides, which the Italian theorists of the sixteenth century did not even consider as architecture (with the exception of Serlio, who lived in France). Thanks primarily to Mansart, this private architecture is now regarded as one of the most important branches of municipal planning. Bourgeois building, which replaced the sumptuous patrician *palazzo* by the *hôtel particulier*, created the network of communications which linked the great monumental buildings and emphasized their importance. The orderly succession of bourgeois buildings, often linked to one another, and distinct from one another only in the different designs of their sober façades, also gave a feeling of perspective to the streets. If the great monuments cause the passer-by to stop and stare, these unpretentious buildings, which although aligned uniformly are not monotonous, seem to accompany him on his walk. They may not claim his attention, but they give him the sensation of moving in eminently civilized surroundings. To leave the center of the city with its grandiose perspectives, and to move into the bourgeois quarters, is like quitting a ceremonial *salon* filled with high officialdom in all its gala finery, for a private room in which ostentation is regarded as in the worst possible taste, and where great elegance is equated with great simplicity. A result of this bourgeois building, which soon spread all over northern and central Europe, was that the middle-class citizen came into direct contact in his private life with the life on the street. Instead of rich and poor districts, there were elegant and humble (often squalid) streets. The severe design of this architecture, with its repetitive façades, was—as an expression of the rising middle class—as representative in its own way as the monumental architecture. But its values were different: comfort, respectability, elegance in the home. It too aimed at influencing a way of life by persuasion and education. For there is a restrained rhetoric of the bourgeois, just as there is a grandiose rhetoric of the Church and State. And in painting these two develop on parallel lines: the grand rhetoric of the historico-religious, decorative-allegorical painting, and the small, subdued but always intentionally persuasive rhetoric of the still life or genre painting.

1

THE CAPITAL CITY

The structure of the capital city, determined by the new political function of the State, went far to shape the seventeenth-century conception of space. In the capital city, modern man does not live in familiar, unchanging surroundings; he is caught up, rather, in a network of relations, a complex of intersecting perspectives, a system of communications, a ceaseless play of movements and countermovements. His position in this articulated space, whose limits are beyond his ken, is at once central and peripheral; similarly, on the "world stage," the individual is at once protagonist and supernumerary. The social influences underlying this new space have been analyzed in masterly fashion by Lewis Mumford in *The Culture of Cities* (New York, 1938).

"Behind the immediate interests of the new capitalism, with its abstract love of money and power, a change in the entire conceptual framework took place. And first: a new conception of space. It was one of the great triumphs of the baroque mind to organize space, make it continuous, reduce it to measure and order, to extend the limits of magnitude, embracing the extremely distant and the extremely minute; finally, to associate space with motion. . .

"The centralization of authority necessitated the creation of the capital city . . . The consolidation of power in the political capital was accompanied by a loss of power and initiative in the local centers: national prestige meant the death of local municipal freedom . . . After the sixteenth century, accordingly, the cities that increased most rapidly in population and area and wealth were those that harbored a royal court: the fountainhead of economic power. About a dozen towns quickly reached a size not attained in the Middle Ages even by a bare handful: presently London had 250,000 inhabitants, Naples 240,000, Milan over 200,000, Palermo and Rome, 100,000, etc.

"Law, order, uniformity—all these are special products of the baroque capital: but the law exists to confirm the status and secure the position of the privileged classes, the order is a mechanical order, based not upon blood or neighborhood or kindred purposes and affections but upon subjection to the ruling prince; and as for the uniformity—it is the uniformity of the bureaucrat, with his pigeonholes, his dossiers, his red tape, his numerous devices for regulating and systematizing the collection of taxes. The external means of enforcing this pattern of life lies in the army; its economic arm is mercantile-capitalist policy; and its most typical institutions are the standing army, the bourse, the bureaucracy, and the court. There is an underlying harmony that pervades all these institutions: between them they create a new form for social life—the baroque city . . .

"Not alone did the new fortifications remove the suburbs and gardens and orchards too far from the city to be reached conveniently except by the wealthier classes who could afford horses: open spaces within were rapidly built over as population was driven from the outlying land by fear and disaster, or by pressure of enclosure and land-monopoly. This new congestion led to the destruction of medieval standards of building space even in some of the cities that kept their medieval form and had preserved them longest . . .

"Power became synonymous with numbers. 'The greatness of a city,' Botero observed, 'is said to be, not the largeness of the site or the circuit of the walls, but the multitude and number of inhabitants and their power.'

"Capitalism in its turn became militaristic . . . Do not underestimate the presence of a garrison as a city-building agent . . . Along with the barracks and drill grounds, which occupy such large sites in the big capitals, go the arsenals . . . The army barracks have almost the same place in the baroque order that the monastery had in the medieval one; and the Parade Grounds—the new Champ de Mars in Paris, for instance—were as conspicuous . . . Turning out the guard, drilling, parading, became one of the great mass spectacles for the increasingly servile populace: the blare of the bugle, the tattoo of the drum, were as characteristic a sound for this new phase of urban life as the tolling of the bells had been for the medieval town. The laying out of great *Viae Triumphales*, avenues where a victorious army could march with the maximum effect upon the spectator, was an inevitable step in the replanning of the new capitals: notably in Paris and Berlin . . .

"The avenue is the most important symbol and the main fact about the baroque city. Not always was it possible to design a whole new city in the baroque mode; but in the layout of half a dozen new avenues, or in a new quarter, its character could be re-defined . . . The military parade had its feminine counterpart in the capital: the shopping parade . . . The old open market, while it did not disappear from the cities of the Western World, henceforth restricted itself largely to provisions: it was only in the poorer quarters, like the Jews' market in Whitechapel, that one could still pick up a dress, a pair of trousers . . . The display market for goods already made, rather than produced on the order system, had already come into existence: from the seventeenth century on, it gradually encroached into one line after another, hastening the tempo of sale and placing a premium upon the visual enticement of the buyer . . .

"The new plan distinguished itself from the older medieval accretions by the use of straight lines, regular block units, and as far as possible uniform dimensions; and the new order is symbolized in the roundpoint with its radiating streets and avenues, cutting impartially through old tangles or new gridirons."

THE CAPITAL CITY

1. Unknown Master: Pope Sixtus V's Plan of Rome, 1589. Fresco in the Sala Sistina, Vatican Library, Rome.

2. Christopher Wren: Project for the Reconstruction of London, 1666. All Souls College, Oxford.

3. Filippo Juvarra: The Piazza San Carlo in Turin, 1721. Print. Museo Civico, Turin.

4. Turgot's Plan of Paris: The Place Royale and the Bastille.

5. Turgot's Plan of Paris: The Invalides.

6. Aerial View of St Peter's, Rome, with Bernini's Colonnade.

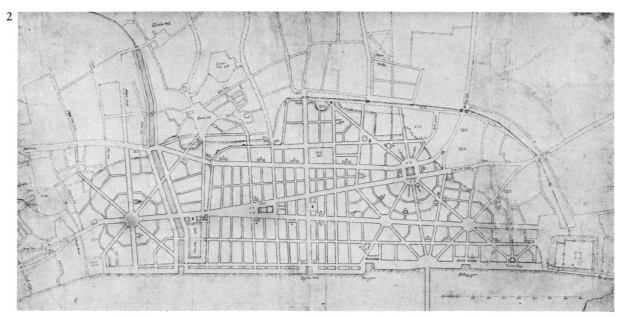

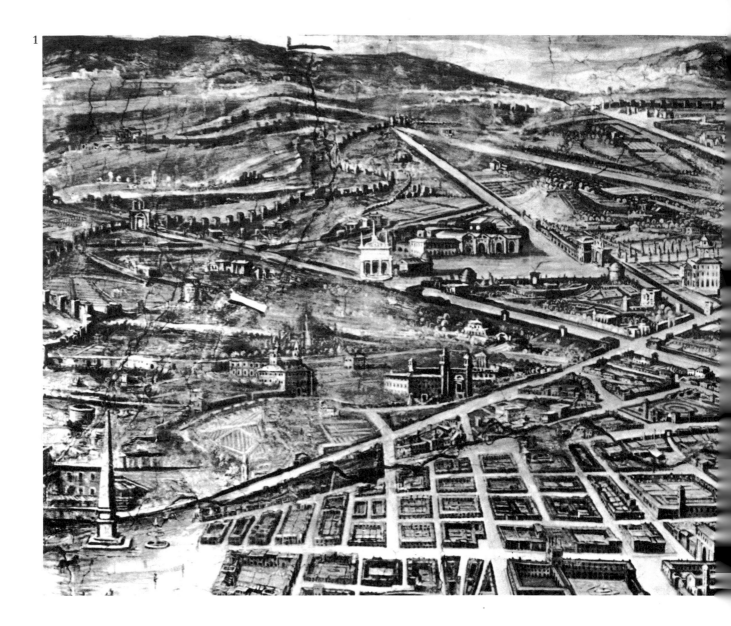

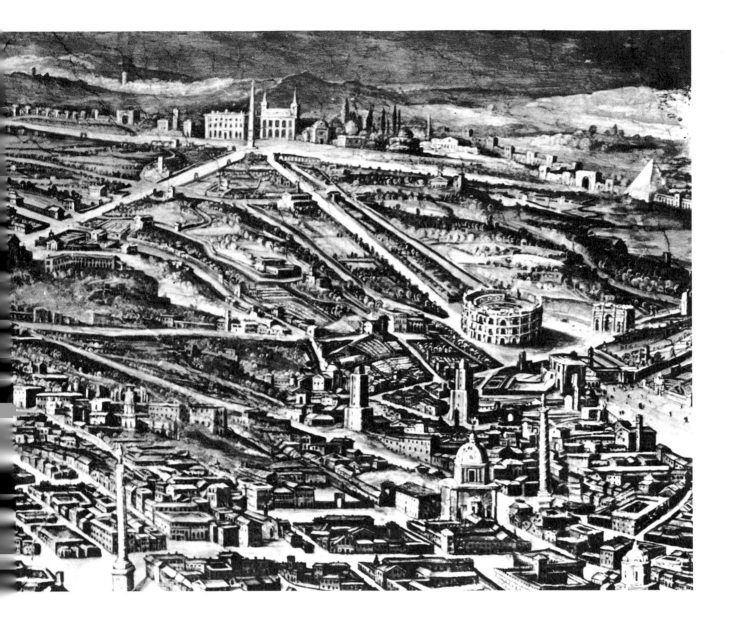

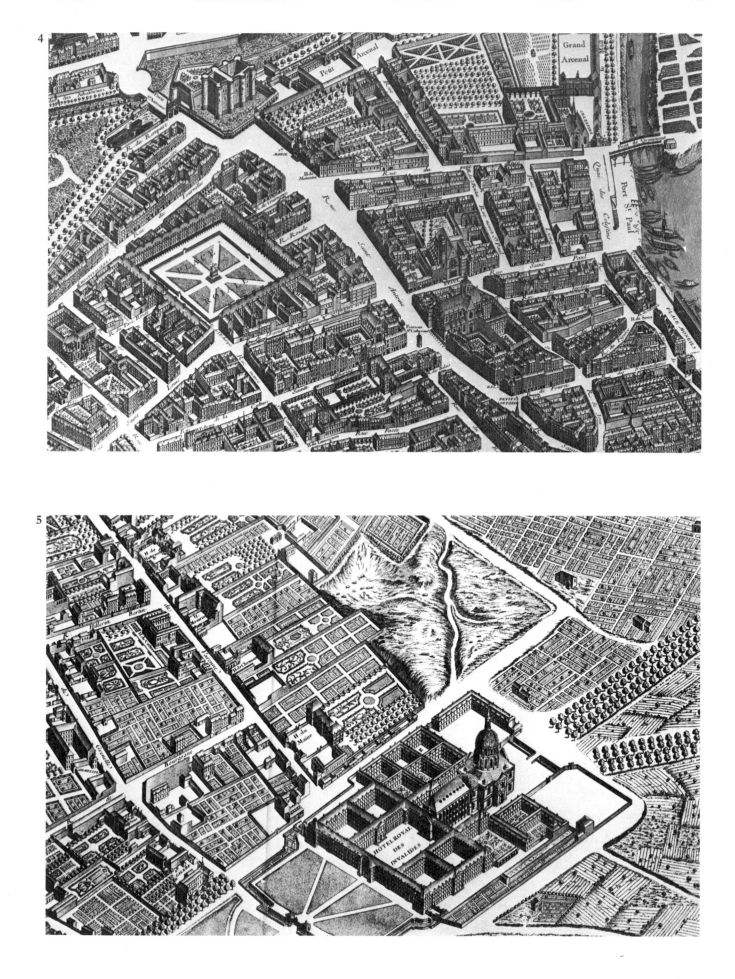

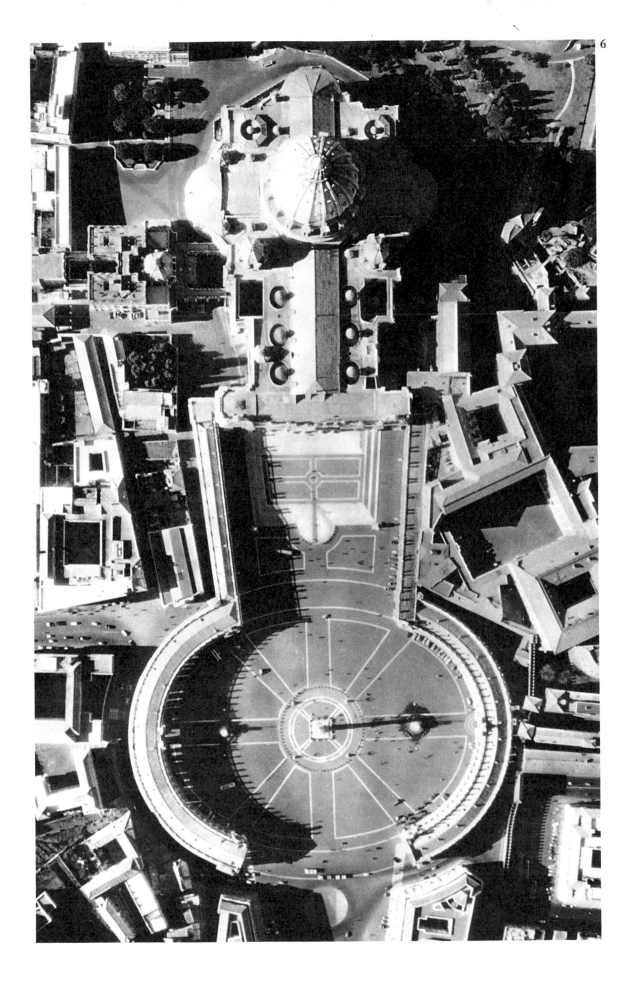

THE MONUMENT

The idea of the monument as a sculptural and architectural unit, representative of values and authority, having therefore a rhetorical or persuasive function, is connected with the idea of the capital city, just as the latter is connected with the idea of the absolute State. The monument forms within the capital city a nucleus of the highest prestige, and it is generally at the center of a vast area laid out so as to give it prominence. The idea of the monument as an expression of ideological values is basically a classical one, revived in the sixteenth century.

The typical monument is the Basilica of St Peter's in Rome, whose construction, which is inseparable from the development of the ideological theme, lasted throughout the sixteenth century, reaching its highest point in the design of Michelangelo, who made the building an organic whole summed up in the synthetic and symbolic form of the cupola. From the first designs of Bramante until the completion of the building, the history of the construction of this "monument of monuments" wavered between two building demands which had to be reconciled: on the one hand, a desire to make it a representative symbol, and on the other, a functional requirement which, in the last resort, was also representative because the religious rite, with its spectacular setting and pageantry, was not only a means but the very substance of the cult. This double intention was already evident in Bramante's designs. He unified the symbolic and the religious function in his synthesis of a central and a longitudinal plan, which were inspired respectively by the temple and the basilica of the classical past. In his vast project Michelangelo again united the two functions, which however appeared distinct and co-ordinated in the final phase of construction, when Michelangelo's central unit was extended on the east side by the long nave designed by Maderna. This decision was made at the height of the Counter-Reformation, and this last solution used the basilica as an instrument for influencing the masses, not without an element of propaganda, but based on the idea that the community of the faithful, or rather the union of Christians, formed the body of the Church, and did not only watch the religious rite, but took part in it.

The long nave added by Maderna undoubtedly destroyed the dramatic unity of Michelangelo's tumultuous mass of masonry, but it also prolonged the basilica into the urban area, thereby developing the urban function of the monument. Later Bernini, by adding the colonnade to the church, and studying its connection with the municipal center, carried even further forward the notion of the monument not only as the pivot, but as a vital center in the municipal complex.

What Bernini, working at the height of the Baroque period, reverted to and developed in the open space of the colonnade, was the form and symbolism of Michelangelo's cupola. The latter is opened out and amplified in the colonnade, just as its original symbolic meaning is amplified by the more accessible allegorical meaning of Bernini's square. The symbol, whose esoteric significance could only be grasped by the initiated, was, by being changed into an allegory, transformed into a demonstrative statement. But the closed form of the round cupola—closed in a plastic and symbolic sense—is implicit, even visually, in the open and elliptical form of the colonnade, whose allegorical purpose, shown in one of Bernini's designs, was to form the arms of an ideal body, of which the cupola was the head. The universal embrace of the Church was therefore the preparation for a supreme revelation and, when we remember that the portico of the Early Christian basilicas was destined for the catechumens awaiting baptism, it is a clear allusion to the people who had not yet been admitted into the Christian Church, but were preparing to enter it. In designing his cupola, Michelangelo was consciously vying with the cupola which Brunelleschi had added to Santa Maria del Fiore in Florence, and which Alberti had described as "spacious enough to cover the heads of the entire Tuscan population." But Michelangelo was determined to give his cathedral a higher ideological value than that of Arnolfo di Cambio's cathedral, which was an expression of the community spirit of the Florentines. Michelangelo aimed at embracing all Christians, and the artist intended that his cupola should be worthy of this end. Bernini intended that the Church should open its arms to contain the whole of humanity. With this allegorical content the "type-monument" reconciles both authority and persuasion and does so under three aspects: as a unitary plastic form, since it is intended to reveal the universality of an ideal value; as an allegorical form, since it not only alludes to but explains the ideological theme; and as an urban form, since it opens out, develops and articulates the "holy" monument in the living space of a "holy" city.

Bernini's summons to Paris to redesign the Louvre reveals that Louis XIV intended to give his own residence a representative and ideological value similar to that of the great Roman monument. But he was dealing here with a royal palace and not with a basilica; and the ideological allegory of Bernini was inapplicable to the purely political theme. The failure of Bernini's project was not due to the King, who highly appreciated the designs of the Italian master, nor to Bernini himself, who agreed on several occasions to modify his plan, always on the lines of what we would call today a "demythification" of his forms. The responsibility lies with a government which, on the specious grounds of economy, preferred the solemn alignment of Perrault's colonnade —an alignment which produces the effect of a troop of soldiers in uniform, on guard at the palace. Against this "governmental" architecture, the King built at Versailles, in the form of "court" architecture, the building which was destined to have far-reaching consequences.

It is significant, however, that in France, as incidentally in Piedmont and a little later in Germany, architecture should have been considered as a "governmental art," organized through official academies and the bureaucratic careers of the architects themselves, who henceforth were part of the apparatus of State, obeying the State's directions for buildings which were largely utilitarian. This explains why the imaginative faculty which, according to the Roman theorist Bellori, is the primary quality of the artist, was less appreciated in France where architecture became above all a form of public service; there the "universal" imagination gave place to the "social" imagination. Mansart, Le Vau, and Perrault were above all highly qualified technical bureaucrats for whom the advantages of utility prevailed over all other considerations, and who did not trouble themselves with "higher" ideals impossible of fulfillment in this world. For this reason, French Baroque architecture was not concerned with giving form to a universal conception of the State. At least in theory it renewed the classical types; but in order to adapt them to practical necessities, it created an architecture in keeping with the demands of public administration.

In Spain and in Southern Italy, particularly in Naples and Sicily, the pomp of sculptural or pictorial ornament was exaggerated; but no attempt was made to deal with fundamental structural problems. The result was a work of great richness, but one whose aim seems to be to overwhelm and impose upon the spectator rather than to persuade him. It is understandable that this phenomenon is to be found in socially and economically backward countries, where authority took advantage of religious fanaticism in order to oppose any form of progress which might be considered politically dangerous. To influence public feeling in this way, the ceremonial and the ritual took on a festive character; and the over-elaborate decoration is no more than an illusion, or a fiction, of richness. In this way the monument has more ostentation than demonstration, more suggestion than persuasion.

In contrast to this, we find in England, after Cromwell's revolution, if not before, a break between the monarchy, discredited by the insubordination of the feudal and landowning aristocracy, and a social and political reality which witnessed the transfer of the control of the country's economy to the middle classes, who were soon to undertake the great task of transforming everything into industrial production. Undoubtedly St Paul's dominated the urban plan of the commercial and financial center of London, just as its extremely high dome dominates the municipal landscape in an authoritarian manner. But there is no ideological aim behind it; if this imposing church impresses us, it is due to its purely secular ideals.

The conception of the monument as a visible form of the historical and ideological values on which traditional authority was based was responsible not only for the structure of the churches and *palazzi*; the urban plan itself, whether rectilinear or star-shaped, was regarded as a monumental symbol, quite apart from its function as a means of setting out the buildings in "monumental" perspective. The geometrical regularity of the layout of Turin, after its reconstruction in the Baroque period, reflects the contemporary desire to resurrect the Roman *castrum* plan, as much as to produce a piece of orderly town planning.

The big squares and principal streets were deliberately planned on a monumental scale. A typical example of this is to be seen in the Piazza Navona in Rome. Its dimensions and perimeter can be traced back to the Circus Agonalis of Roman times; and its designers, Rainaldi, Borromini and Bernini, were clearly influenced by its historical associations. Bernini, the creator of the great "Fountain of the Rivers" in the center, gave it an historical-allegorical quality, by uniting natural elements (the waterfalls and rocks) with allegorical elements (the statues), and with the palm (which is both a symbolic and a naturalistic motif).

If we agree that the city, as an entity, can be regarded as a monument, it is clear that special importance must be attached to the means of entry. Its gates are no longer merely openings in the walls, but symbols of its illustrious past, having something in common with the triumphal arch of classical times. Further, they symbolize the distinction (which was becoming daily more evident) between the country or suburb, and the center, or historical nucleus, of the city. The social structure was changing, and a clear distinction between the city-dweller, whatever his class or income, and the countryman was appearing.

The notion of the monument soon became a part of everyday life and began to influence the decoration, ornaments and furnishing of civil as well as religious buildings. In the *palazzi*, we find monumental courtyards, staircases, galleries and salons. They are no longer simply the homes of the ruling classes, but a part of the ceremony and ritual of an ostentatious social order. The churches now possess altars, pulpits, funeral monuments, organs, pews for the worshippers, even confessionals, which are in themselves monumental ornaments. The altars have something in common with the doorway; they are framed by orders of columns, surmounted by one or more tympana, and give access as it were to the imaginary space of the tabernacle or reredos. In St Peter's, in Santa Maria della Vittoria, in the altar of the Blessed Albertoni in San Francesco a Ripa, Bernini defines the space behind the altar as a part of heaven, where the miraculous apparition takes place in a supernatural light, unconnected with the light of the rest of the church.

Bernini had a flair for theatrical effects, and he regarded a funerary monument as a form of allegorical representation or "triumph," an excuse—as with the Baldachin of St Peter's—for transforming a place of burial into a grandiose monument, with the aid of imperishable materials. Implicit in his notion of the monumental tomb was a double, and seemingly contradictory, meaning; on the one hand, sorrow at the departure of its illustrious tenant from this life, and on the other, joy at his arrival in heaven. This allegorical theme naturally required the presence of many figurative and architectural elements; for an allegory tends to enlarge or generalize the event it depicts.

It is easy to understand how this monumental form, which became increasingly connected with the habits and way of life of the seventeenth century, soon spread throughout Europe. The taste for the monumental, with its reference to the classical past, suited the ruling classes, who regarded themselves as divinely ordained to exercise authority and power. The "grand manner" (which is no more than an extension of the notion of the monument to all domains of art) thus became identified with the tastes and culture of the conservative class—which in turn explains why the middle classes began to produce, in rivalry, their own particular form of art. It is because the monument now became a class symbol that we see, for the first time, specific aspirations, tastes, even ideologies, being identified with different social classes.

The problem linking Baroque architecture with an attempt to make authority and power visible in a monument is even more acute in the peripheral zones of the Catholic world, in the colonial architecture of Mexico, Brazil and Peru. In the pagan or recently converted countries of the New World, persuasion was a form of propaganda, and the problem was to explain the doctrine and morals of the Catholic Church by using the imagery of the natives as much as possible, and by asking them to be its interpreters; for in general the missionaries did no more than provide a summary plan of churches to be built, while the construction and decoration were left to local artists. The "contamination" of pagan and Christian iconography has nothing paradoxical in it, at least in so far as the less important themes are concerned. Apart from one or two symbolical motifs, a free hand in decoration was given to the natives. They used this privilege to cover the interior and the exterior of the buildings with a profusion of colors, of gold and images, which often portrayed the barely concealed survival of a pagan cult based upon the offering of flowers, fruits and votive objects.

The Baroque architecture and decoration in Latin America are exactly the reverse of what we find in the "monument." Their forms have no metaphysical import, they reveal no transcendental values, symbolic meanings. Here allegory is fable or apologue, and exaltation of the spirit belongs only to the popular fiesta, while religious education can be carried out only through songs and dances. The sacred iconography of Christianity is, for the most part, a travesty of pagan imagery. In this way, the popular and traditional ebullience, which was quite spontaneous in the craftsmen, was retained, thanks to Baroque design, together with a kind of elementary joy, a feeling of liberation when contrasted with the nightmares of an archaic, oppressive and bloody religion. However indirect this contact may have been with the culture of the West, it gave birth to a popular art recalling all the variety and color of folklore.

2

THE MONUMENT

In the "Dictionary of Architecture" by Quatre-
mère de Quincy, the notion of the "monument"
is connected with that of the public building: the
church, the royal palace, the town hall, the law
courts, theaters, schools, etc.—in fact with the
notion of the "embellishment and magnificence of
the city." But he adds that often we find "simple
private people who have made their own houses
into monuments, such are the grandeur and magnificence which they have lavished on them." The
fundamental quality of the monument is its representative function. It always possesses an ideological
content and meaning, and because it aims at
representing the stability of certain ideal values, it
is always expressive of the principle of authority
and its historical basis.

It is therefore understandable that the monument
tended to be seen as something ancient, evoking
classical forms, even if it is a purely symbolical
classicism having little influence on the form or the
practical function of the public building in the
seventeenth century, when the authority of the
Church was identified with its active religious
function, and that of the State with its administrative
function and government. Its architectural effects are
achieved by the employment of certain "classical"
elements, such as the cupola, the column, the
pediment, etc. Little purpose would be served by

seeking a concrete symbolical content in these forms, which had long been out of use and forgotten; the aim of the monument is to use these symbols as vague conceptions of representative architectural forms, without specifying what they really represent. Because they have a representational value they must, above all, be visually imposing. This explains why, in the seventeenth century, the purely visual effects of a building were more important than its actual construction. In this way, the ancient identity of static construction and plastic representation of space was destroyed.

One of the most representative forms was the cupola, its prototype being the cupola of St Peter's in Rome, which ideally represented the authority of the Church, dominating and protecting the world. In the seventeenth century almost every church possessed its cupola; their domes emerged high above the roofs of the city and gave its distinctive character to the new urban landscape. Nor should we forget that the church had a parochial role, as the essential administrative unit of the Baroque city. If we compare various cupolas, we see that they have no exact or prescribed form; some are higher than others, some lower, some more graceful, more flattened, more attenuated or more bulbous. Broadly speaking, their form is determined by the shape and size of the building and the character of the urban landscape. When Longhena built the Church of the Salute in Venice he had in mind the form of the nearby cupolas of St Mark's. Defying tradition, his church has two identical cupolas because St Mark's has many, and this kind of volumetric repetition is characteristic of the urban scene in Venice. The cupola of the Invalides in Paris is high and narrow, supported on an elongated drum, and joining up with the whole body of the building; it is the Baroque version of pointed Gothic architecture. The cupola of the church of

St Paul's in London is none other than an "official" symbol, a sign of authority, as symbolic as the Queen's crown. The same can be said of the columns. They have no structural function, and are purely representative; the insignia of power and authority. As such, they can be repeated vertically or horizontally, aligned or superimposed, isolated or grouped together; they often possess the value of a dominant motif, of a recurring musical theme. As simple symbols of power, they were adopted even in private architecture, for no other reason than for their "representative" value, as indicating the stability of the English social system, as betokening rank and wealth. As vague allusions to authority, they are to be found everywhere; in the corridors of palaces, in the altars of churches, in monuments to the dead.

A separate phenomenon, indicative of the first rupture between the sovereign and the public administration, was the appearance of the "royal residence" outside the city. The king wished to distinguish between his private house and personal style of living, including his court, and his official position as head of the government, symbolized by the royal palace which remained his official residence in the city. Versailles is an example of this. It was the seat of the court; here the palace is surrounded by a huge park, laid out so that it seems to be directly connected with nature. The sovereign was the first official of the state, for which he carried out the prescribed duties; but he was also a "privileged nature," bound by mysterious ties with God. His court was an élite society, and his worldly Olympus a well-ordered, well-disciplined Arcadia, obedient to his sagacious government. The garden or park was the place where the man who was first in the social hierarchy could look out beyond it and become a part of all creation.

THE MONUMENT

1. Libéral Bruant: Hôtel des Invalides, Paris, 1671-1676, with the dome by Jules Hardouin-Mansart, 1679-1706.

2. Baldassare Longhena: The Church of Santa Maria della Salute, Venice, 1631-1687.

3. Christopher Wren: St Paul's Cathedral, London, 1675-1710.

4. François Mansart: The Church of Val-de-Grâce, Paris, 1645-1665, with the dome by Gabriel Le Duc.

5. François Blondel: The Porte Saint-Denis, Paris, 1672. Sculpture by Michel Anguier, 1674-1676.

6. Louis Le Vau: Hôtel d'Aumont, Paris, 1645. Later additions by François Mansart.

7. Louis Le Vau and Jules Hardouin-Mansart: The Garden Façade of the Palace of Versailles, 1679-1684.

8. Antoine Coysevox: The Passage of the Rhine, bas-relief in the Salon de la Guerre, Palace of Versailles.

9. Antoine Coysevox: The Tomb of Cardinal Mazarin, 1689-1692. Louvre, Paris.

10. Claude Perrault: The Colonnade of the Louvre, Paris, 1664-1668.

7

9

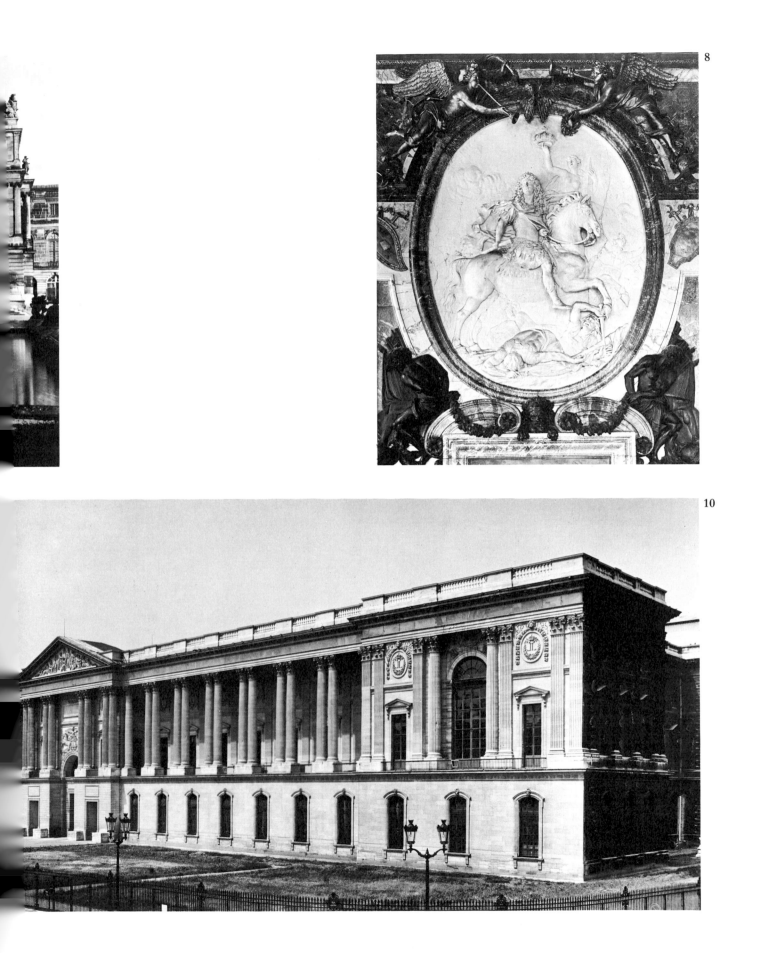

THE MONUMENTAL

The sense of the monumental is connected with the historical-ideological character of the monument itself, and with those accumulated values which are to be found in the capital city; but it has a far wider range and gives rise to almost limitless phenomena, with an immense variety of aspects. The idea of the monument, which took form in the sixteenth century, especially with Michelangelo, is inspired by the humanist conception of the statue as the transposition or evocation of a "memorable" figure, in keeping with the universal view of history. The statue is also a *monumentum*, that is to say an object which recalls and designates in a past which is already "historical" a model or example to the present and the future. When Bramante, in designing the new basilica of St Peter's, sought to make it a "monument," he wanted to give tangible plastic form to an idea, but he based his design on the Pantheon and the Constantinian basilica because history alone is able to sanction the universal and imperishable value of an idea. To express the monumental in the seventeenth century meant to express oneself in a universal manner, that is with a feeling for grandeur and with scorn for the "detailed" or modest: to follow in fact what was called throughout Europe the "grand style." But every artistic undertaking (whether in painting, in sculpture, or in architecture) carries with it a unilateral experience, which on its own cannot lead to the universality of the grand manner. This is always, and cannot be otherwise than, the result of a convergence or meeting (but not of a synthesis *a priori*) of painting, sculpture and architecture.

During the development of the problems raised by the construction of the new St Peter's, the theme of the monument broadened to that of a feeling for the monumental; this can be seen in the way Bernini, while creating his colonnade, transformed Michelangelo's symbolical motif of the cupola into an allegory. But he did something more. He felt that the monumental value of a building cannot be born in the imagination or intellect of one man alone, that it is created and ripens slowly in the collective consciousness. In his plan for the final complex of the buildings, he wished simply to harmonize these different and even contradictory ideas (the central place of Michelangelo's transept, the longitudinal position of the nave of Maderna closed off by the rectilinear façade), but to order all these solutions in a perspective which was to be more ideological than spatial. The cupola, which is a symbol of supreme spiritual authority, defines the space where the ritual takes place, enacted by those who are invested with the authority to guide and persuade the worshippers; the long nave is the space set aside for the worshippers and for those who are persuaded, for those who represent the present reality of the mystical body of the Church; the colonnade is the place for those who wait, who look to the future and are themselves the future of the Church. The intersection of the nave and transept is covered with the ideal Platonic heaven of the cupola; but above the open space of the colonnade is the "natural" cupola of the physical sky, because humanity which awaits the revelation here is still in a state of nature. Lastly, the form of the monument is the meeting place in the present for the authority of history, which is transmitted by the memory of the experience of the past, and for the possibilities of the future, which belong to the imagination. The arbitrariness of this prototype is corrected by imagining the future as history or anticipated memory; in this way, the past too is imagined rather than remembered, because it is none other than the desired form of future events.

The normal language of the "monumental" is allegory. It is not allegory as it was imagined in humanism, and which consists in explaining meanings which are hidden beneath the appearance of the phenomenon or of the image; the problem here is to translate abstract conceptions into visible form. Because it is universal, the conception expresses itself in extremely generalized images situated in a universal space, and in an indeterminate time. Moreover, this presupposes that the process of allegory is a typical process of art, and because art is a fiction, allegory is, properly speaking, the fiction of art which, basically, is all allegory. We find artistic creations which can be called "allegory types," because they have the appearance of an allegory even if their conceptual content is not precisely stated. The frescoes of Annibale Carracci in the Farnese Palace, for example, are of the allegory type, because they represent scenes taken from Ovid's *Metamorphoses* and therefore have a naturalistic-mythological content; here the process of allegorization is inseparable from that of the fiction of art. The different parts of the pictorial presentation are distributed in architectonic frames which are decorated with monochrome herms acting as caryatids. Here we have a clear distinction between, and combination of, the three arts: painting, sculpture, architecture. The setting is simulated architecture, the caryatids are simulated sculpture, the scenes are *quadri riportati*, that is, easel paintings imitated in frescoes. It is almost a set program in which art imitates art, or more precisely, art imitates the imagination. But imagination already possesses an artistic element, because it is always a means of creating images, of extending mental activity beyond the data of direct experience.

Imagination exists, to a greater or smaller degree, in everyone; but it is only the artist who can translate images created in the imagination into visible images. If this were all, art would be simply a technique capable of revealing a process of the mind; the representation of a representation. But art, as Tasso also said, does not discover, it creates ("art creates everything, nothing is discovered"); and if the artist represents nothing which cannot be depicted in credible form, his manner of imagining is already conditioned by the necessity of manifesting itself through the medium of art. In a word, art shows that a certain means of imagination is translated into an act of creation and that, therefore, imagination is connected with human action, influencing conduct, even morals. The only condition for this is that it passes through artistic creation, which is basically the fact of the imagination. By using his imagination, man can assess in advance the extent of his own action. By projecting his intention into a time and space which are greater than those of the present and the immediate, he places his artistic imagination on the level of the grand style, and his action will benefit by this spatial-temporal enlargement. In using these greater dimensions he abandons himself to fiction; he confers on the action a "monumental" or historical character. Because history is itself an act of the imagination, it ceases to be merely a study of the past, and deals with the more immediate space and time, connected with the practical life, with morals, and politics. The imagination, as defined in the seventeenth century, could only become a political and social imagination. We have already seen how the importance of this imagination, this ability to think of the world and oneself beyond the data of the present and the real, is a fundamental character of the Baroque political outlook.

To understand how the "monumental" tends to surpass all categorical limits, and how the imagination became a manner of life, it is enough to compare Annibale Carracci's decorations in the Farnese Gallery with the great vault painted about thirty years later by Pietro da Cortona in the Barberini Palace. Here too the "monumental" stems from a combination of the effects peculiar to each of the three arts; here again we have simulated architecture and simulated sculpture. But the total effect of the ensemble is pictorial; the sculptures seem to come to life, and the architectural parts are no longer simply frames for the different scenes; they are broken up by figures in movement, by clusters of flowers, vegetation, clouds. In the paintings of the Farnese Gallery, nature has entered only as a complement to the mythological figures, acting as a classical background to a poetically imagined scene; here imagination has produced a second nature, in which trees, figures, clouds, architecture are all seen in a more ample, indeed almost limitless, dimension. But in the work of Cortona there is something new; painting can imitate architecture and sculpture, and does so, but it cannot itself be imitated. Among the arts (which are all "mimesis," that is imitation), it is painting which has the greatest power of imitation; it is the senior art, the one which most directly makes the imagination visible. (Pietro da Cortona was also an architect, indeed a greater architect than painter; but his architecture has pictorial roots, and we tend to see it in pictorial images.) Because the principal aim of art is to make the imagination perceptible, and because painting has, as far as perception is concerned, greater possibilities, the "visual" values of painting, in the first place colors, must be accentuated. This was the contention of Rubens who, when he was working in the first years of the seventeenth century in Rome, had a profound influence on the formation of the Baroque, and specifically on Bernini and Cortona. In this way we can understand how Baroque art, which was born in Rome, was so quick to take advantage of the experience of the Venetian colorists—to the extent that, after the third decade of the century, the home of Baroque art may be said to be, with Longhi, neo-Venetian. The only difference is that color was no longer subordinated to the principles of equilibrium and symmetry, no longer kept within the "natural" limits which had been respected by sixteenth-century painting, even by the highly emotional art of the great Venetian masters. Color now is deployed to the full, intensified, heightened, "monumentalized," simply because, if imagination is something which goes beyond reality, the embodiment of its images must go beyond the norms of visual experience. We may therefore say that to perceive something is not only to register it mentally, but to be solicited by it; the mind must create new systems of reference adapted to the perception of objects which are no longer "natural," but artificial products of man. From this it follows that the true activity of man no longer takes place *inside*, but *beyond*, nature; it is obvious that society, the grouping of men for common aims, is the first great conquest beyond the "natural condition."

The ceiling paintings in the church of the Gesù, by Gaulli, and in Sant'Ignazio, by Pozzo, are respectively forty and sixty years later than Pietro da Cortona's *Glorification of the Reign of Urban VIII* in the Barberini Palace. In the first, by Gaulli, we find no trace of illusionism, not even in the sense of an illusory prolongation of the architecture of the church. The ceiling is wide open; beyond a huge *impluvium*, the sky extends, peopled with angels and saints adoring the rays of Christ's monogram. This is another society which inhabits another space, beyond the society of living humans and the terrestrial space. That this is so, is proved by the fact that some of the figures, suspended on the limits of the cornice or climbing over it, aspire to mount into that celestial space; while others, the wicked, are repulsed and fall down. It is worth noting that the light emanates from the monogram of Christ, which is a symbol, but that it falls and creates a shadow as natural light would. Between the physical space, the allegorical space, and the symbolical space, is a continuity and a progression as between terrestrial life and life beyond the earth. This is the thesis of communication, or of the "ladder," which St Francis of Sales opposed to the Protestant thesis of man's utter inability to communicate with God. Pozzo on the other hand, in the ceiling of the church of Sant'Ignazio, again represents architecture in perspective; but this no longer has any connection with the architecture of the church. Henceforth the society of the elect has its house, its palace and its court in heaven, quite distinct from the space and the architecture of the society of the living, and more splendid, but obeying the same laws of perspective, the same visual logic. It is a visible and plausible view of the world beyond the horizon of experience.

This "sense of the monumental" in Baroque art is none other than the limitless extension of representation into near and distant space, in a time which is at once past, present and future. And clearly nature, as much as history, is a part of this limitless dimension. This is why we also find the sense of the monumental in landscapes, portraits, sometimes even in still lifes.

NICOLAS POUSSIN (1594-1665). THE FINDING OF MOSES, 1638. LOUVRE, PARIS.

The monumental style need not necessarily be grandiose, imposing or theatrical. In spite of its small size and the absence of rhetorical effects, the Finding of Moses *by Nicolas Poussin is a monumental painting; this is so because the scene is represented* sub specie aeternitatis, *as a natural miracle which, repeated cyclically, has taken on the religious significance of a rite. With precise and measured gestures, as if dictated by the rules of a cult, her handmaidens stand in a circle around Pharaoh's daughter, like acolytes around a celebrant. The rite evokes the myth of the Nile. The river is personified in the classical manner by the man lying on the ground, while the water jar and the cornucopia allude to its periodic inundations and the ever renewed fertility of the earth. The landscape, too, is monumental: in its translucent clarity, it has something of the balanced architecture of the distant city. The colors are limpid and firm, without any tonal shading or shrillness; they seem to be carved out by the light, and vibrate on the surface of the painting as on a sheet of water stirred by a breeze.*

In Jephthah's Sacrifice, *Sebastiano Mazzoni achieves monumentality in the contrary way: by movement, and by using perspective devices to expand the picture space and accentuate the lighting effects. The architectural setting, with its perspective foreshortenings and the arcades in the background sharply outlined against the light, promotes the movement of the figures, which is rhythmically accentuated by the marked differences in size between near and distant figures, by the interlinking gestures of the agitated groups, and by the flashing lights in which they move. The effect is frankly theatrical. Charles Le Brun, on the other hand, in* Moses and the Daughters of Jethro, *has given a monumental and historical quality to a simple shepherds' brawl around a country well. The inspiration of this picture goes back to Domenichino and his conception of the "historical style." But, with Le Brun, the effect of monumentality is achieved by transforming the figures and their gestures into "types" of emotion—curiosity, amazement, scorn, rage, fear. To monumentalize, for him, means to decharacterize or generalize; so that even an anecdote can be made into history if it is related according to the rules of the "grand manner."*

SEBASTIANO MAZZONI (1611-1678). JEPHTHAH'S SACRIFICE, ABOUT 1650.
SAMUEL H. KRESS COLLECTION, WILLIAM ROCKHILL NELSON GALLERY, KANSAS CITY, MISSOURI.

CHARLES LE BRUN (1619-1690). MOSES DEFENDING THE DAUGHTERS OF JETHRO, 1686. GALLERIA ESTENSE, MODENA.

GUERCINO (1591-1666). AURORA, 1621. CASINO LUDOVISI, ROME.

In 1613 Guido Reni had painted his Aurora *on the vault of the Casino Rospigliosi, following Annibale Carracci's method of the* quadro riportato *; what we have, in other words, is a fresco painting actually designed as an easel picture. In 1621 Guercino dealt with the same theme on the ceiling of the Casino Ludovisi, but applied the opposite principle of naturalistic illusionism, setting the subject in an architectural framework seen against the open sky. Guercino's theme is the same mythological fable, but it is depicted as a kind of natural prodigy. Here, in the open sky between the great pillars of a vault which has fallen in, the chariot of Dawn rides triumphantly across the clouds. This is not a reversion to some classical theme, but a wholly unexpected apparition whose effect is to cause intense emotion. The illusion is not only visual but psychological ; for if the three foreshortened pillars make the viewer feel the depth of the sky, the shattered pillar on the lower right shows that the vault has fallen in and thus explains why the apparition is visible from within the building. Since the picture space is no longer illusionist but imaginary, the naturalistic motifs (trees, clouds) only make the apparition more convincing. The prodigy is, in fact, presented as occurring not* beyond *but* within *nature.*

Three years later Bernini created the psychological illusion of the Baldachin in St Peter's—a small portable object inordinately enlarged. The shafts are twisted bronze columns which spiral up into space, and the heavy festoons seem to tremble as if stirred by the wind. The great cavity of Michelangelo's cupola appears above, immense and boundless like the vault of Heaven. Later, in the Fountain of the Rivers *in the Piazza Navona, Bernini carried illusionism even further. Not only do the waters pouring from the fountain introduce an intense feeling of nature into a city square, but the rocks and palms evoke the distant countries and exotic landscape in which the rivers personified at the base of the fountain have their source. For Bernini, allegory is a natural process of the imagination ; the images of the human mind are as infinite as the faces of nature, and allegory is therefore nothing more than a way of discovering the possible meanings of reality.*

GIAN LORENZO BERNINI (1598-1680). THE BALDACHIN OVER THE HIGH ALTAR OF ST PETER'S, ROME, 1624-1633.

GIAN LORENZO BERNINI (1598-1680). THE FOUNTAIN OF THE RIVERS IN THE PIAZZA NAVONA, ROME, 1648-1651.

IMAGINATION AND ILLUSION

Aristotle is explicit in the *Poetics*, where he says that we can imagine as possible, probable or credible only things which we know have already happened: the imagination thus has its basis in history. But the precise repetition of an event is improbable, and is a particular case, whereas the object of poetry is the universal. If the representation is to be universal and not particular, the event must not repeat itself by chance, but as a result of certain laws of probability and necessity. The laws of the drama are not logical, they are not dependent on cause and effect. If they were and if, given a certain situation, we were able to foretell the events which would follow, these events would have little effect on the spectator, nor would they be able to arouse in him any feelings of terror and pity—the feelings that drama must arouse (terror at what surpasses his imagination; pity for himself and others). The law of *necessity* exists from the outset in the mind of the artist and establishes the design of his work (it is an *eike*); but the spectator recognizes it only *a posteriori*. This notion forms an integral part of Baroque aesthetics. We find it, for example, in Reni's *Massacre of the Innocents*, where the two themes, pity and terror, are balanced almost architecturally, establishing the Aristotelian unity of time and place, while the angels descending from heaven indicate the moment of catharsis.

The transition of the artistic imagination from the true to the probable or possible can be traced in the spatial or, more exactly, optical illusionism which was already widely practised in the sixteenth century. Not for nothing did the seventeenth century develop and exploit all the possibilities of perspective, which moreover was no longer regarded as a method of construction, but only as a means of representing space. In Bologna there arose a school of perspective painters, the *quadraturisti*—painters who specialized in illusionist decorations based on the virtuoso use of perspective and foreshortening. We may ask ourselves why, if illusionism was so important, it was reduced in the seventeenth century to a specialized branch of painting and practised as a kind of handicraft? Obviously because, in the great arc of the imagination, illusionist painting is only a small sector or, more precisely, an optical or physical moment in a process of development affecting the whole field of human thought.

In his *Aurora* (1613), in the Casino Rospigliosi, Guido Reni rigidly applied the principle laid down by the Carracci, that art should imitate art: his fresco is a *quadro riportato*, an easel picture transferred to the ceiling. Guercino, in his *Aurora* (1621) in the Casino Ludovisi, attempted to surpass Reni by employing another form of illusion, more psychological than optical, though it too is based on visual data. Certain visual effects may have a coherence which means more than formal logic: Reni wishes to demonstrate the Aristotelian thesis of "pleasure in imitation," while Guercino uses imitation as a means of emotional suggestion. Guercino's chariot of the Dawn riding on a cloud is obviously absurd; but the color harmonies, the strong chiaroscuro of the clouds, the light and dark patches on the dappled coats of the horses have a visual coherence which makes the viewer accept unquestioningly what his sense of logic tells him is absurd. Guercino's solution is more "naturalistic" than Reni's. The mythical chariot is seen rolling swiftly across the sky, and by showing that one of the pillars is broken the painter tries to suggest that the vault too has fallen in, thus leaving the open sky visible. To obtain psychological coherence the painter has thus had to break up the logical coherence of the four converging pillars.

In many seventeenth-century paintings the extension of space from the immediate foreground into the remote distance does not mean only a progressive diminution in the size of things; it also involves a change in the quality of things. Certain objects conspicuous in the foreground are depicted with such realism that it seems almost possible to reach out and touch them; while above, in the clouds, are the figures of saints and angels. It is the tangibility of the first which makes the miraculous vision of the second credible. In the moral sphere, it is our direct experience of the real world which enables us to believe in things that transcend reality; and this often by contrast, for it is the cares of daily life that predispose us to believe in the eternal bliss of the hereafter. The art of the seventeenth century was intended to take effect in the moral rather than the intellectual sphere. Space and time are elastic rather than limitless; their extent and duration are continually changing. In a painting such as the *Miracle of St Ignatius*, Rubens uses perspective foreshortening to depict the man possessed by a devil in the foreground; behind, on the steps, kneel the devout imploring grace; at the altar the saint invokes divine intervention; and from on high appear the angels whom the saint has summoned to his aid. The sequence of events in time has been conveyed by a sequence of figures in space. If the term "illusionism" must be used, it is well to note that in this case the artist creates the illusion of time by means of space.

The illusion may also be in things themselves. Zurbaran depicts a female saint as a Spanish gentlewoman dressed with a dignified elegance befitting her exalted social rank. He evidently intended with this social metaphor to allude both to the privileged rank of the saints in the hierarchy of spiritual values and, at the same time, to the spiritual value of the social aristocracy. The sumptuous garment is a means of illusion (and of persuasion), since it serves to establish the mental correlation between a social value and a spiritual value.

In Bernini's baldachin in St Peter's, in Rome, we have a typical case of psychological illusionism. Attempts had been made to erect a ciborium—a small temple, one might almost call it—under Michelangelo's dome; but every architectural structure appeared insignificant in such surroundings, dwarfed by the mighty pillars of the church. Bernini did not proceed by reducing a piece of architecture to a small scale. He took a relatively small object, a processional baldachin, and enlarged it enormously, transforming the slender shafts into ponderous, twisted bronze columns. A great innovator in all scenic effects, he thereby achieved a mental illusion

founded on a reversal of our usual notions of things. We normally think of a building and a processional baldachin as being out of all proportion to each other. A building reduced in size merely gives the onlooker a sense of being cramped. A baldachin greatly enlarged compels the onlooker to alter and extend the scale of sizes to which his eye is accustomed. This is the effect Bernini sought to obtain.

The artist recognizes, then, that all scales of values are relative and that space has no fixed dimensions. He means to range freely over all metrical scales, and this explains how a painter can give us a nearby still life and an otherworldly vision in the same picture. But if there are so many scales of sizes for the different categories of objects, space is no longer created by the "uniformity" of proportions, but by the relations between disparate things. Thus it is that in this multidimensional space, we discern particularities which had no place in the classical conception of space; and each thing, while forming part of a grandiose, universal whole, preserves its quality as a thing in itself—just as, in the varied and active intercourse of society, the distinctive character of each individual, far from being obscured or lost, is brought out all the more clearly.

In the field of town planning and urban architecture, this conception of space led to a continual variation of size relationships, to the use of different scales, to attempts to achieve visual surprise, to a change-over from the restricted perspective of the street to the broad expanse of the square, to an unexpected view of a monument and the sudden opening of a vista. But it also led to the typological differentiation of buildings in accordance with practical requirements; and it meant that certain structural elements, like the façade of a church or an arris that links up two perspectives, were carefully studied and worked out with great precision. In the two churches in the Piazza del Popolo in Rome, for example, Bernini broke up the classical symmetry intended by Rainaldi, by transforming the round cupola of one of the churches into an ellipse in order to bring it into line with the perspective axes of the two streets; and by using the corner of the church as the pivot on which the perspective turns, he gave it the same value as the portico in front.

This new imaginary space, which art uses as real space, has not only dimensions and proportions but also direction. Generally speaking, perspective no longer serves to mark the position of a motionless onlooker, but supposes a moving onlooker and follows his physical and optical movements along a multiplicity of changing lines of sight. In the process allowance is made not only for the objective conditions of vision, but also for the psychological factor. To take a typical example in Rome. Borromini's church of San Carlo alle Quattro Fontane and Bernini's church of Sant'Andrea al Quirinale are both built on an elliptical plan. But our feeling on entering the first is one of spatial contraction or constriction, while in the second we have a sense of spatial expansion. This effect is caused in part by the architectural structure, which is disproportionately large in the first, and small in the second. But more than this, the effect is achieved because the main axis in San Carlo runs from the entrance to the altar, while in Sant'Andrea it is perpendicular to the altar; so that the space which appears laterally compressed in the first appears expanded in the second. Obviously the axis running from the entrance to the altar is the one most favored as a spatial determinant, because it is along this axis that one normally enters a church. The development of space is therefore studied in relation to a normal condition of vision, but in both cases it violates or breaks visual habits and alters the "normal" estimation of distances and sizes.

It is well known that the Baroque aesthetic aimed at producing illusion and exciting wonder, and clearly it achieved the second by means of the first. But we know today that illusion, as a psychological no less than a visual phenomenon, is not so much the extension as the alteration of a "normal" condition, and that it is this alteration which produces the emotional shock which in turn arouses our sense of wonder. In the case of the two churches mentioned above, the contraction or expansion of space excites wonder because it modifies the usual symmetrical layout of the circular building, and thus balks our psychological expectation of symmetry.

IMAGINATION AND FEELING

The emotional shock caused by the rupture of normal visual conditions does not cause an eclipse or a dispersion of visual values, but on the contrary their intensification. Because the image is no longer conditioned by equilibrium, by the symmetrical compensation of nature, it is subject only to the limits of verisimilitude and possibility. But this, too, is only relative, because even the image most divergent from experience is "possible," by the very fact of its being translated into something which is objectively existent. In this sense, there is no contradiction between the "natural" imagination of Bernini and the "unnatural" imagination of Borromini, or of Guarini. They are simply two different methods or processes of the imagination.

The emotional shock intensifies the activities of the senses, but it cannot have positive effects on the intellectual faculties. From the point of view of knowledge, all illusions are false. But, as we have seen, the aim of persuasion is not truth but what is useful. If what is true has a contemplative value, then what is useful has one of inspiration. So that astonishment before any work of the marvelous is an experience which must be assessed above all by the yardstick of action. In the view of Descartes, feeling does not belong to "rational" nature, but rather to the "mixed" nature of man. It is preceded by a moment of thought, when the viewer is confronted with a factual situation; after this comes the reaction (pleasure, pain, etc.), and this is followed by an action (approaching or departing from the object, etc.). To the extent that feeling causes or solicits action, it betrays a lack of satisfaction with the present. We wish to have a profounder knowledge of what we are observing, or to leave it or, more positively, to change it. Our imagination places us in a situation which is different from the one we are in physically, but it is feeling which controls our choice of the many imaginable situations. And rhetoric, which directs a situation selected by choice, is in control of the domain of feeling.

An emotional speech will be more persuasive because it involves the listener, will make him share the feelings of the orator, or at least arouse in him similar emotions.

The positions can differ, but only within these limits. Caravaggio confines himself to presenting the fact as a sudden happening, without inquiring into its causes or envisaging its effects; but the same light which reveals it to us, fixes it irrevocably and displays its "gravity." This "gravity" does not suggest the attitude which must be taken, but it creates a state of reponsibility. In the face of facts, man is free to act as he wishes, but he is aware of what is irrevocable in the facts, and of the corresponding relative responsibility for himself. Rembrandt, on the other hand, makes a profound study of the motives behind the facts; not in the sense of what has caused them logically, or as a cautionary tale, but in bringing out the possibilities, the secret motives and the deeper impulses which have determined human action in the past, as they do in the present. Velazquez, who was the most lucid of the seventeenth-century painters, overcomes the conflicts of past, present and future, claiming in a sense complete freedom to assess reality in his own way, but at the same time recognizing the necessity of taking a definite position, of reacting actively to every situation. Poussin considers history as a closed dimension, in which everything is "beautiful," because nothing can be modified by present contingencies. The human condition is therefore only a feeling of expectation with regard to history (not unlike that expectation of phenomena which is Giorgione's and the early Titian's feeling towards nature), even if this sense of expectation is sustained by a melancholy certainty that the future, too, will become the past beyond the bounds of death. Rubens on the contrary turns the experience of the past and the imminence of the future into an exciting feeling, which is intensely vital, of the present. But if feeling determines human action, there must also be the possibility of directing it. This was the task assumed by the artists who followed in the wake of the Carracci, notably Guido Reni and Domenichino, and whose work, diffused over a wide area, gave life to all forms of "official" art.

If feeling is essentially man's "natural" reaction, and is therefore always to some extent the feeling of nature, it is not possible to transform natural feeling into social feeling unless the problem of nature, and therefore of the "beautiful," has first been settled. The chief function of the art trend typified by Guido Reni is essentially the transformation of natural beauty into moral or social beauty. These artists accepted the verdict of history as to the beautiful: this meant Raphael and, within limits, Titian. Here was an elect nature which no longer presents any problems, but which simply defines the ideal condition of man in the world. His adventure in the world, that is to say his reactions to the situations it presents him with, has yet to begin. Beauty is that ideal condition in which all relations with nature can be achieved, and which founds a state of equilibrium or measure. It is the form in which disordered passions are composed in a harmonious system giving place to ordered actions. Guido Reni's *Atalanta and Hippomenes* is a search for the beautiful, but the beauty of the two figures is felt only in the clearly geometrical equilibrium of their movement. The best way of controlling feelings is to be aware of them, and to classify them; to arrange them according to categories or types is also the way of defining their "general" or social values. Guido's painting is almost a repertory of types of feeling. The various Davids represent youthful self-assurance; the saints at prayer, devotion; the Magdalens, contrition; the Lucretias, virtue taken

to the point of self-sacrifice; the Cleopatras, the pangs of love or fidelity to one's affections; the Hercules, victorious strength, and so on. Whether intentionally or not, these figures are allegories; the figures stand for concepts or for types of feelings, but the reference to mythology or to ancient history shows that the category is not an abstract one and has its roots in history. The figures are "beautiful" because they reveal a nature which from the beginning is one of the elect and educated. The "beautiful soul" is the new title of nobility to which all men may aspire, even if they are without illustrious antecedents. The education which creates the "beautiful soul" is not learned through precepts nor from historical examples. Education is achieved as a result of persuasion. In so far as the "beautiful" is considered as action or suffering "beautifully," or as an invitation to allow oneself to be persuaded, it can be found as much in men as in women, as much in the young as in the old, or in children. The "beautiful" ceases to exist as a formal category, and is succeeded by corporeal and physical types. The various temperaments and feelings correspond to as many expressions of face and gesture. More accurately, we may say that we are dealing more with the characteristic than the beautiful; but then characteristic features are generalized into "types of character," to which is added a moral judgment. Murillo identifies moral beauty with the innocence of childhood, which is also the image of faith in God. Ribera, with his ragged philosophers, rehabilitates the ugly in order to demonstrate the value of true wisdom which despises worldly goods. Rubens and Jordaens no longer see any reason for separating ideal beauty from sensual beauty, even in historical-religious or allegorical scenes. Van Dyck openly associates elevated feelings with the privileged social classes.

3

THE EMOTIONS

Lomazzo, in his "Treatise on the Art of Painting, Sculpture and Architecture" (1584), identifies the expression of feelings with the movement of figures: the painter who is best acquainted with the mechanics of the human body and its movements will best represent its inner movements, the emotions. In the seventeenth century, however, the artist's intention was to communicate an emotional state, to cause a sentimental response in the spectator, rather than to represent the feelings and their corresponding physical movements. Thus, in the scene represented, there had to be something inconclusive which tended to linger on in the mind of the beholder. Mochi depicts his *Veronica* in one of the niches of the great pilasters of St Peter's; he sees her at the moment when she tears the veil away from the face of Christ and becomes tremulously aware that it bears the imprint of his features. It is clear that even the monumental presentation of the figure has an allegorical meaning: it is an image of the Church which conserves the living imprint of the Redeemer. For this reason, the face has a generic or mask-like quality, beautiful, mournful, wonderful; there is nothing pitiful about the gesture, it is in keeping with the monumentality of the figure, which occupies the whole space of the niche transversely. The inclination of the head to the other side accentuates the movement of the diagonal lines of the drapery, causing them to converge towards the veil. What in fact the artist intended, was to create a sense of increasing and mounting rhythm, transforming the folds of the dress into so many lines of force flowing towards a peripheral vertex, at the extreme limit of the space, thereby suggesting a prolongation and continuation of the movement.

Too much has been written about the ambiguous character, half-mystical half-erotic, of Bernini's *Ecstasy of St Teresa*. It cannot be denied that, among the many religious themes of seventeenth-century art, one was the transposition or sublimation of the erotic into an almost physical love of God. But a psycho-analytical examination of the work would not take us beyond this thematic motif, which was very frequent in contemporary lyrical poetry and religious literature. In Bernini, moreover, the theme has a more immediate *raison d'être*. It may be described as the renewal, in the manner of the Carracci so congenial to Bernini, of Correggio's aesthetic of the sensibility. Bernini suspends his plastic group beyond the altar in a small chapel or shrine which possesses its own source of light and is thus distinct from the rest of the church. All the forms are melted and fused together by this light; the clothes of the saint are a bright palpitating mass, fully alive, and those of the angel swirl like a flame (allegorically: a blaze of love, as if the angel were the visible embodiment of the saint's ecstatic vision of love). The faces, hands, and feet are simply points of extreme luminous intensity in an animated mass of light which extends to the clouds and communicates its radiation to the whole of the surrounding space, thereby evoking a flow of emotional sympathy in the spectator. For Morazzone, however, mystical ecstasy is a death struggle; what is *eros* for Bernini is death for him. Here we have the two poles of the Baroque attitude to life. Morazzone was a Lombard whose religion had the pietistic strictness of the faith preached by St Charles Borromeo. The difference between him and Bernini is essentially thematic; in Morazzone everything melts into shadow rather than light; only one last, livid ray of light illumines the tortured and consumed face of the saint. Here too the sentiment, the pathos, is not conveyed by a gesture, a movement, an action, but by a contraction or convulsion which occupies the whole of the space. Representation is reduced to the minimum in order to intensify the sense of entreaty and spiritual stimulus. What the artist wants to do is identify the spectator with the suffering of the saint, to make him feel at least a part of the martyrdom.

The position of Ribera is very different. His *St Sebastian* is a carefully arranged figure, like a model who has taken the pose. Even in the throes of martyrdom it retains the elegance, even the grace, of a gesture which—we see it in the right hand—is more demonstrative than expressive. The saint's body is that of a splendid nude, drawn according to the rules; but in order to show that the figure is real, and its sufferings real, the painter has added to the nude the realistic detail of the hair on the chest and in the armpits. The face, its eyes raised to heaven, is that of an actor singing a solo aria. The painter plays his tricks openly and makes no attempt to conceal the scenic artifice; he probably realized that, in order to evoke a sentimental reaction, theatrical devices are no less effective than crude reality, perhaps even more effective. He has recourse to every expedient. The martyr has a boyish youthfulness, and only his short beard gives his face a certain virility. His pose is artificial but harmonious; in the foreground we see his flank transfixed by an arrow, an almost brazen appeal to the compassion of pious women. Here the seventeenth-century public is being prepared for and acclimatized to "useful" fiction.

THE EMOTIONS

1. Francesco Mochi: St Veronica, 1629-1640. St Peter's, Rome.

2. Gian Lorenzo Bernini: The Ecstasy of St Teresa, 1645-1652. Santa Maria della Vittoria, Rome.

3. Morazzone: the Ecstasy of St Francis. Castello Sforzesco, Milan.

4. Jusepe Ribera: St Sebastian, 1638-1651. Museo Nazionale di Capodimonte, Naples.

PERSUASION AND DEVOTION

Persuasion attempts to obtain a way of life, a *praxis* in conformity with the principles of authority; the means for this is communication, which is not a one-way movement only, from top to bottom. St Francis of Sales saw in devotion not so much a bond as a "ladder" which leads from earth to heaven. God may grant spiritual and temporal grace, but man must ask for it with prayer.

The devotional image had already appeared in Late Mannerist painting, its aim being to give a tangible object to prayer. In the seventeenth century it became an instrument of devotional practice, and a genre of historical-religious painting. It was always connected with a special kind of devotional practice, sometimes with special prayers; its function was to exhort rather than to represent or to glorify; and for the purposes of repetition and propagation it was simplified.

The Council of Trent had confined itself to condemning "licentious" nudes and prescribing the ways in which the painter could better serve the Church: he was called upon to instruct the people and confirm it in the faith, to show it the gifts lavished upon mankind by God, to edify it with the vision of miracles, to induce it to follow the example of the saints. At the center of the debate was the question—maliciously raised by Aretino—of the nudes in Michelangelo's *Last Judgment*. But very soon, quite apart from the alleged irreverence of such figures, they were judged by the canons not only of religion but of taste. In the opinion of Gilio, *devotional* figures are the reverse of violent figures (the reference to Michelangelo is obvious); the devotional picture should accordingly be "faithful, pure, true and chaste." In other words, it is the very reverse of a violent and dramatic composition. In this discussion reference was even made to the serenity of the Primitives and, following Vasari, the example of Fra Angelico was invoked. In 1564, after much argument for and against Protestant

iconoclasm, René Benoit defined the function of images in his *Traité catholique des images et du vray usage d'icelles.*

In the seventeenth century, besides reforming the traditional iconography and thus opening the way for a new effort of the imagination, the Church was engaged in a propaganda campaign which had the effect of rapidly fixing the iconography of the new saints, since their example was frequently invoked as a guide and stimulus to others. To combat heresy, which denied the cult of the saints, it wished to demonstrate to all the faithful, even to the most humble, that the way to heavenly glory was open. More than heroes, confessors, masters, and martyrs of the faith, the saints were now teachers and advocates. In every case, they were intermediary figures who maintain the contact between life on earth and the Heavenly Master. To attain salvation, and yet to have lived at the same time in this world, the help of God with all His Grace is required for every act on earth. With their eyes looking to heaven, the palms of their hands open towards the earth, the saints invoke Divine Grace, and dispense it to the faithful, or entreat God to accept their prayers. Even figuratively, the devotional image is a compromise; it evokes the traditional physiognomy of the saint, idealizing it vaguely into the "beautiful," in allusion to its condition of beatitude. The nobler attributes are indicated with precision, while the others are neglected. The setting is reduced to a few allusions to life on earth, and to the celestial domain which the saint has reached; for this reason the coloring and lighting, also "generalized," are vaguely suited to the theme, and aim rather at influencing the feeling of the devout than fixing the image in a purely structural form. The goal, in fact, is not in this case to excite surprise or to stimulate imagination, for the soul of the devout believer is then deep in prayer, and it must not be troubled by an image which might distract it. The image is, in fact, conceived for a purely auxiliary or instrumental function, the simplicity of its style making it immediately familiar. Communication here makes no call upon the intelligence; it takes place on the "subliminal" level, as we would call it today. Unlike the great scenes of religious history which attempt to create a state of lively astonishment, the representation of devotion tends to induce a feeling of humility in the devout believer, the only suitable manner in which to address God. The tone of the visual communication is humble, fervent, insistent. Deliberately avoiding a brilliant style, recourse is usually had to a language which it would be excessive to call archaic, but which can certainly be called artificially "old-fashioned": this is the case in Italy with Sassoferrato, and in Spain with Zurbaran. Because the visual approach is to be only a guide and almost a whispered suggestion to the devout person at prayer, the choice of a humble and often old-fashioned language in no way excludes the use of other familiar forms of speech; dialect and vernacular terms are to be found in the devotional images of Ludovico Carracci, and they are even more marked in other Bolognese artists, such as Guercino, Guido Reni, Centino. At Naples, in the paintings in the Hermitage of Camaldoli, Gramatica produced scenes in a frankly popular vein, which translate the sermons of Lent with the aid of lifelike figures. The artistic level of devotional pictures is often almost intentionally modest; typical of this period was the development of a popular art encouraged and guided by those in authority, and widely diffused by means of prints for propagandistic and devotional purposes. However, when the tone is elevated without borrowing its rhetoric from scenes of history, sometimes a truly religious lyricism is produced. This is to be seen in the austere images, free of Murillo's unctuous quality, of Philippe de Champaigne, who adopts a severely classical diction, in the Poussin manner, but does so out of purely Jansenist rigor and shows no interest in the imagery associated with the classical style. It can be seen even more in the greatest "lyricist" of the seventeenth century, Georges de La Tour, who, influenced by Caravaggio, achieved a strict archaism which puts him beside the great masters of fifteenth-century French painting.

GEORGES DE LA TOUR (1593-1652). THE MAGDALEN, ABOUT 1625. LOUVRE, PARIS.

Some of the greatest artists of the seventeenth century appear to have been at variance with the "spirit of the century" and are often regarded as anti-Baroque painters simply because they did not take a conceptual view of art and had no imaginative exuberance. They examined reality very closely, looking for a new meaning in things, an interior religious quality unconnected with conventional piety. This explains why the problems of the time were often reflected in their work more consciously and clearly.

Almost all the paintings of Georges de La Tour have an internal, distinctly localized source of light; but his aim was certainly not to study the science of "particular lighting." It would be truer to say that he set himself the problem of reducing space to the small zone illuminated by the ray of a candle or an oil-lamp. The figures, often screening off the source of light, define the picture space and form precise volumes of light and shade. Even faces and objects become geometrical forms and luminous volumes. In short, La Tour does not admit any a priori conception of space; he rejects perspective illusionism and does not even consider the possibility of a space existing beyond the small aura of light in which his figures are placed. He saw space only as a means of situating an event, a human figure, or a group of objects.

In experimenting with light effects, La Tour was exploring a field which had been opened up in the very first years of the century by Caravaggio. In the Supper at Emmaus, the figures are only screens defining the luminous zone revealed by the reflection of the white napkin, which is lit up by a shaft of light falling from some invisible source. The painter wished to focus attention on the objects on the table, whose shapes are emphasized by heavy cast shadows: these are the real subjects of the picture. And the gesture of benediction (the beardless Christ may be a self-portrait, and the picture a polemical statement, the "manifesto" of Caravaggesque realism) has more than a religious meaning; it proclaims that all things in the real world are of equal value because each of them embodies the ultimate problem of being and non-being, of life and death.

That this was the case is to be seen in one of Caravaggio's loftiest, most tragic and polemical paintings, the Death of the Virgin. *Here again the light falls from a definite but invisible source on to the body of the dead woman and the shoulders of the weeping Magdalen. The figures of the Apostles on the outskirts of the luminous zone transmit the rays of light; they stand motionless, nor is there any space beyond their silent presence. Of reality, the artist seems to say, all we know is that part of it which transpires in an event in which we ourselves are humanly involved. We cannot escape or elude it, for our existence is wholly bound up in what happens here and now.*

But strictness does not exclude devoutness. In the Supper of St Charles Borromeo, *Crespi expresses the meditative concentration of the saint by contrasting the objects on the table—which are also symbols of poverty and penitence—with the bareness of the room. Whether the theme is death or ecstasy, the problem is the same: the presence of things is revealed by the absence of man. But there is one artist who eludes this tragic dualism: Velazquez. In the* bodegones *which he painted in his youth, he took up the themes of Caravaggio, but without recognizing any hierarchical distinction between man and the objects around him. Figures and objects, for him, have the same value and are not mutually exclusive. Each of us is, in fact, the product of our own experience, and we do not need any abstract process of thought to identify ourselves with the things which enter into our daily experience and consciousness. Objects do not have any hidden meaning; they are in a sense a part of ourselves, a counterpart of the ego.*

Caravaggio's Death of the Virgin *was rejected as an altar picture because it was considered blasphemous or irreverent. It was neither "holy" nor "devout"; but that it was a profoundly religious painting was implicitly recognized by one of the most pious Catholic painters of the seventeenth century, the Spaniard Zurbaran; he borrowed its composition and lighting for his* Funeral of St Bonaventure, *a work not only devout but inspired by the strictest ideals and precepts of religious orthodoxy.*

DANIELE CRESPI (C. 1598-1630). THE SUPPER OF ST CHARLES BORROMEO, ABOUT 1628. SANTA MARIA DELLA PASSIONE, MILAN.

CARAVAGGIO (1573-1610). THE DEATH OF THE VIRGIN, 1605-1606. LOUVRE, PARIS.

CARAVAGGIO (1573-1610). THE SUPPER AT EMMAUS, ABOUT 1595. BY COURTESY OF THE TRUSTEES, NATIONAL GALLERY, LONDON.

DIEGO VELAZQUEZ (1599-1660). THE OLD COOK, 1617-1622. NATIONAL GALLERY OF SCOTLAND, EDINBURGH.

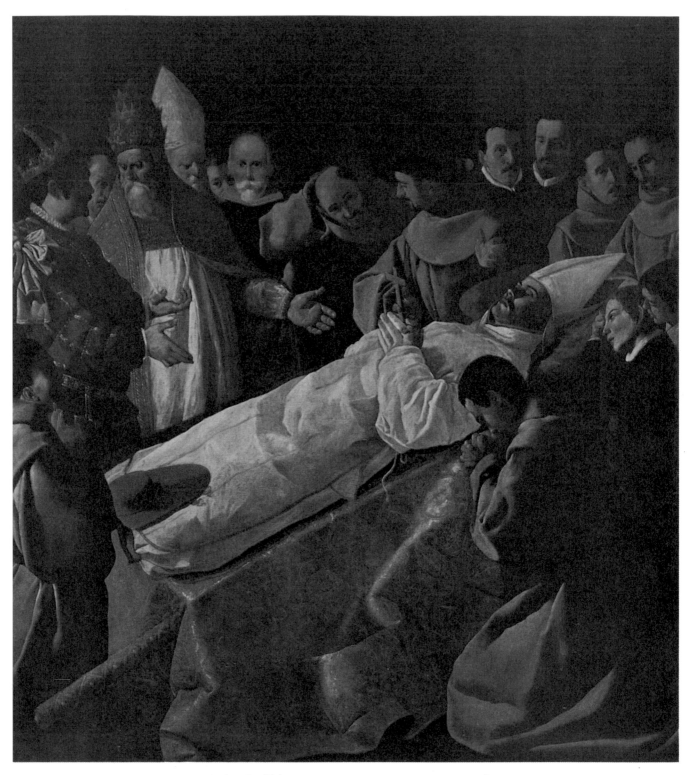

FRANCISCO ZURBARAN (1598-1664). THE FUNERAL OF ST BONAVENTURE, 1629. LOUVRE, PARIS.

The contrast between inner piety and its outward forms, between true feeling and mere display, is to be seen again in architecture. Protestant churches are bare and unadorned, places of prayer and self-communion; those of the Counter-Reformation are monumental and ornate, symbolizing in all their forms the universal authority of the Catholic Church. A Dutch painter, Pieter Saenredam, depicted the interior of St John's Church in Utrecht as a vast, empty space containing a few, small human figures lost in prayer. But the sanctity of the place is conveyed by the soft light from on high falling through the great windows, skimming over the barrel vault and glowing on the bare walls. In the great void of the world, he seems to say, man is alone; but he is comforted by the light of God.

The Roman architect Carlo Rainaldi built a votive church, Santa Maria in Campitelli, in which an image said to work miracles against the plague was venerated. The "spiritual" plague of the day was the Protestant heresy, and the collective cult of the mass was considered the best defense against the dangers of a purely personal religion, lacking the discipline of the established Church. Rainaldi's church encloses a vast, light-filled area whose structure is reduced to the plastic articulation of the walls. In Baroque architecture, every structural element had an allegorical as well as a spatial meaning. The pilasters and columns allude to the sustaining power of the faith, but demonstrate its truth by creating a space calculated to impress on the faithful an ideal image of the order of the universe. Thus the light which in Saenredam's picture fills the entire space here illuminates the massive columns, the moldings of the arches and entablatures; it forms a great sea of light under the cupola and subsides into the penumbra of the side-chapels. The whole church is designed to make the most of the play of light among the structural members. And the great empty space of the interior is, in the last analysis, an allegory of nature as reflected in the civil forms of architecture.

PIETER SAENREDAM (1597-1665). INTERIOR OF ST JOHN'S CHURCH AT UTRECHT, 1645. CENTRAL MUSEUM, UTRECHT.

CARLO RAINALDI (1611-1691). THE CHURCH OF SANTA MARIA IN CAMPITELLI (INTERIOR), ROME, 1663-1667.

RHETORIC AND CLASSICISM

The crisis of classicism coincided with Mannerism, while the Baroque was a revaluation of the historical and naturalistic experience of classicism. The new feature of the seventeenth century was that the classical canons were placed in antithesis to a new, realistic approach to art. The antithesis became perceptible in the first years of the century in the painting of Caravaggio; it developed later in the antithesis between Caravaggio and Carracci, which was noted by the critics, especially Mancini and Bellori. They contend that Caravaggio despised the teaching of the ancients, and that his painting resembles nothing which had been done or thought before, nor does it resemble nature, for natural actions call for development or exposition, while Caravaggio records an actual moment in all its arresting immediacy. The antithesis therefore is between a painting which implies speech or language, described by the classical principle *"ut pictura poesis"*; and on the other hand a painting which has no contact with poetry, which is only painting, or pictorial *praxis*. Classicism, as language and speech, is demonstrative, and thus classical representations have a beginning, a development and an end. Classicism is therefore historical and natural, because it gives us the "natural" development of actions, while realism, in spite of its professed fidelity to truth, is unnatural and unhistorical, because it represents an action as a mere occurrence, without explaining its causes or consequences.

But this antithesis is too schematic. It is true that Caravaggio, following the old advice of Leonardo, did not study the ancients, and attempted to record things with an unflinching directness and immediacy, as they actually took place. But even the critics of the seventeenth century recognized the link, in the first phase of his work, which connected him with the Venetian masters of the sixteenth century (Zuccari, for example, commented on the "Giorgionism" of his *Vocation of St Matthew*); and it is clear that during his Roman period he proposed

a new interpretation of Michelangelo. Nor can it be denied that, against Mannerism, Caravaggio stood for a return to nature, even if nature for him is not the mistress of experience, but at once a spur and an obstacle to moral commitment. In the same way, Borromini followed Michelangelo's example, not in imitating his forms, but in conceiving of art as an ever unsatisfied aspiration towards transcendence, going beyond considerations of "finish" and formal perfection. Caravaggio, as much as Borromini, interprets the master in a rigorous, essentially moral fashion, very different from the literal interpretation of the Mannerists or the eclectic borrowings of the followers of the Carracci.

These last, incidentally, were soon to extend their condemnation of the Michelangelesque Mannerists to the master himself. Their admiration went to Raphael and Titian, in whom they saw a harmonious synthesis of idea and experience and, even more, a serene confidence in those supreme values of nature and history which Michelangelo, in his ceaseless desire to surpass himself, had called into question, and even denied in the last phase of his career. Guido Reni and Domenichino, working within the vast stylistic current initiated by the Carracci, took up again the Mannerist theme of the idea, but they identified it with the art of Raphael rather than that of Michelangelo: the "beautiful," or perfect harmony between man and nature, belongs to a past which can be contemplated but cannot be recovered in the present, which corresponds with the feelings and anxieties of the moment. As feelings are projected into the future, as expectation or anxiety, so they are projected into the past, as nostalgia for some good which has been irremediably lost. Even for Poussin the classical world is a world from which he felt himself cut off, and for this very reason it appeared to him more beautiful and attractive, even though its quiet harmony bears such a resemblance to death we cannot consider it without a profound sense of melancholy. And how can we fail to notice in the greatest landscape painter of the seventeenth century, Claude Lorrain, a feeling for nature as of some lost boon, a happy realm into which one longs to escape.

The classicism of the Carracci and of Bernini, with its derivatives, is undoubtedly nearer to life. Antiquity was a time when human history, having as yet no otherworldly aspirations, was carried on entirely in nature. It is therefore impossible to separate nature and history, impossible to abandon the allegory which shapes ideas into natural images. But if this is so, the natural character of the human being and his feelings can only be revealed in a domain where the classical identity of nature and history is recognized. It is only beyond these limits that the domain of the possible opens, a perspective which the Christian faith has revealed to men as placing the goal of life beyond life itself.

Rubens goes even further. Human feelings, the "passions of life," no longer know limits of time; they no longer possess a past, a present, or a future. The images of the past, evoked by memory or passed down by history, and also those of the imagination, press down on the images of the present, which the senses perceive, and are so vivid and concrete that they finish by coalescing with them. The antithesis, which appears later in the quarrel between the followers of Rubens and Poussin, was founded on their opposing conception of classicism, the sense of myth, of nature, of history. This is not to say that Poussin does not feel nature with an emotion which is sensory; he expresses it, in fact, with all the intense coloring of the great Titianesque tradition. But for him nature has come to a standstill, and the message which its images transmit is the message of another time, of the past, which has been consigned to history. The structure of the landscape is the crystallization of a reality which has existed and which exists no longer. Rubens' composition, on the other hand, is dynamic, a turbulent accumulation of masses, while his colors surge like endlessly breaking waves. The future and the past do not dissolve, but intensify feeling; they hasten the possession of the present in which the feelings play a part. Rubens' themes—myths, history, nature, allegory and faith—are not very far from those of Poussin, but his conception of them is different; that is, the interpretation of classicism, which had defined these great values and which remains after

all the foundation of art, differs in the two painters. There is between them a divergence of tendency (as in Italy between Caravaggio and Annibale Carracci, between Borromini and Bernini). In the seventeenth century the development of art took place in terms of conflicting tendencies, which form with their dialectical tension the unified web of the culture of the epoch. These tendencies do not consist in different attitudes towards nature, but towards history. And history, in the seventeenth century, is still the history of antiquity. The Neoclassical phase which succeeded the Baroque confined itself to reducing the tendencies and the different interpretations of the "classic" to a sole, official form founded on science, and not on the free interpretation of the antique.

The debate on the meaning and the value of history, or of classicism, can be reduced to the antithesis between a positive and a negative interpretation. Either history is the basis of experience, of our confidence in the future, of life itself; or it is a past to which there is no return, the object of hopeless regrets, death itself.

The problem of life and death, which was of vital concern to all, could not be considered without reflecting on the values of classicism and history; for the problem changes according to whether it is regarded in terms of nature or society. The theme of death, overt or hidden, is present in all Baroque art. It is conspicuous in the monumental tombs in which allegory triumphs. It is conspicuous too in the funeral decorations which theatrically accompany death and mourning, with the same ritual pomp as that of marriages, feasts, coronations. We need only observe the macabre symbolism of these *castra doloris* to realize that the rhetoric of death attempts to "denounce with overpowering luxury the vanity and the grandeur of luxury" (Chastel). This fantastic interest in the pomp of death has equally a social cause—it is necessary to show to the people who have to submit to the wishes of the great of this earth, that these men too will die, and will have to render their account to God of the authority that, thanks to Him, they exercised on earth. The powerful man leaving this world is greeted with all the honors which are his due, but we are ignorant of the fate which awaits him after the Judgment of God in the "just" society beyond the grave. Nor does he go there immediately. First comes his death, then burial, then the decomposition of his body, the break-up of that marvelous machine which the anatomists could now describe in all its detail. If life has a close connection with nature, death can take its place easily in the same harmonious cycle, and there is nothing terrifying about it. But if the horizon of life is bounded by society itself, to die means to drop out of that society, leaving behind uncompleted undertakings, which will be either taken up by others or abandoned. The very ambiguity of this funereal symbolism reveals that all this ritual is an alibi, a fiction to draw a veil over the horror of death. This *public* representation of death merely removes the fear of individual death, of this experience which each must face alone.

Caravaggio had the temerity to tear away the veil of fiction. This man who despised history as ordered in a logical sequence, and shows more interest in the event as it happens, sees in death the "true" event with neither cause nor effect. Death is not a passage towards another life; it is the violent encounter with reality beyond the deceptive curtain of nature. After physical death, we do not enter into celestial glory, but into the obscurity, the cold, the loneliness of the tomb. This fearful emergence of death is the price he pays for his scorn of the classics. But that the classics can no longer teach a man to live (or to die) according to nature is to be seen in two pure classics, Poussin and Claude Lorrain, in whom tragedy is dissolved in elegy, and horror in melancholy, but the dominating thought remains the thought of death. The same can be said even of artists endowed with brutal vitality, such as Rubens, Jordaens, Frans Hals. They reduce everything to the present, to the instant; but for this very reason the problem of what goes before and what comes after is frightening, evoked by the orgiastic explosion of life. It could not be otherwise. Once the equilibrium of humanity and nature was broken, it was necessary to enlarge, to twist, even to contradict and break up the structure of the classical form, in order to adapt it to its new context; the relationship between the present and history becomes even more tense and precarious, and only very few artists are capable of overcoming the contrast between modern life and ancient history, or of framing their own work in a "modern" history. These are the same men who seemed to go beyond the limits of the Baroque by illuminating its true meaning in this, the first century of modern Europe.

The idea of "modern" art (to which Bellori also alludes in the title of his "Lives") implies taking up a new attitude towards history. History is certainly the only dimension of life, because it is defined by the life lived by humanity, but it is no longer a rational construction laid down by providence, nor the earthly source of authority; it is a succession of events in which it is impossible to distinguish a governing hand. Bernini and Pietro da Cortona, relying on the imagination, described a perspective which seemed probable or lifelike; but they were well aware that their view of the future as an image of the past was a mental illusion translated into a visual illusion. It is impossible to eliminate chance; and by admitting chance, we have at best the art of the Bamboccianti, the low-life painters, who recorded what they saw in the streets. But if we put aside the notion of rational history, the question is not whether we accept or refuse chance; if chance is a part of human destiny, the problem is to prepare the mind to face it, and to define at any moment and in any situation the conduct which must be followed. If art is persuasion, the problem is not to persuade others of this or that, but to assume a clear and logical attitude before this or that, before everything that exists. This need of a new humanism, a humanism which brought with it in a century of political servitude a new *dignitas hominis*, was felt by those artists who were most acutely aware of the historical situation as a "European" situation. It was not Caravaggio or the Carracci, whose art remained "Italian," even if its influence was felt all over Europe; it was not Poussin, even if his classicism is metahistorical, just as his nature is metaphysical; nor was it Rubens, in spite of the cosmic and universal character of his vitality. As for the antithesis between Caravaggio and Carracci, between Borromini and Bernini, between Rubens and Poussin, we have already seen that it is limited to their different but univocal interpretations of classicism. The great antithesis of the century is that between Rembrandt and Velazquez; and it brings into play, from two opposite poles, the culture of the Reformation and that of the Counter-Reformation.

The two artists possess a "European" culture. Rembrandt is, directly or not, related to Caravaggio, the Venetians, Rubens and, through Elsheimer, the Germans up to Dürer. Velazquez is connected with Caravaggio, El Greco, Rubens, the Venetians, the Bolognese masters of the seventeenth century and even with the ancients, whom he studied critically, especially during his second journey to Italy (1648). Behind Rembrandt was the religious skepticism of Bruegel. To break through this skepticism and arrive at an ethical attitude, as Rembrandt wished to do, means to reduce experience, to discern the underlying motives of history in what may seem to be a disordered accumulation of events. The painter had a great humanist culture; he was friendly with the Jews of the Amsterdam synagogue, and spiritually akin to Spinoza in his pantheistic conception of things, although in a moral and not a naturalistic or animistic sense. God does not govern the world because he is *in* the world, immanent though intangible; he lives with men, he takes part in their affairs. It is only this secret presence, this perpetually renewed passion of God, which gives a logical sequence to events, and which creates history. History then cannot be a selection of memorable events; how could it be, when compared with the infinity and eternity of God? All painting, in so far as it can depict anything, is historical painting; but the function of history, and of historical painting, is not to exalt but on the contrary to diminish, to minimize the value of human actions, so that human pride does not conflict with or eclipse God. Of all human actions, the only one which does not offend or hide God is suffering; God himself came down on earth to teach men to suffer. The figures of Rembrandt do not act; they suffer the light and the shade, space and time, life, things themselves. Therefore, although God is also in us, and to recognize Him is to recognize ourselves, we must always recognize ourselves in others. Once we have overcome our first disgust, even the carcass of a flayed ox appears tragic, worthy of pity, full of sadness and suffering spirituality, like a Christ on the Cross; and not because of the symbolic association but because of a deep identification. If we can humble ourselves to the point of finding our own reflection in this flayed ox, or in the corpse lying on the dissecting table in the *Anatomy Lesson*, we shall discover not only ourselves but God. There is no judgment in Rembrandt's reading of life, therefore there is no catharsis; the only attitude to adopt, the only "historical" action, is to suffer what the world inflicts and to resign ourselves to reality. The individual will is not suppressed for the benefit of authority, for God who is everywhere present in the world does not delegate authority to anyone to govern in His Name. If authority no longer reposes on Divine Power, it is arbitrary, absurd, a sin; and without authority there can be no persuasion. This, in fact, is the great truth which Rembrandt discovered—that there can be communication among men without involving persuasion. For this reason Rembrandt, although resigned to man's fate, is also a rebel, at least as regards the authority of the ancients. His conception of history, as the story of man's suffering and not of his glory, made him particularly dear to the Romantics, to Delacroix for example, and to Fromentin, who was the first to understand him.

If behind Rembrandt is the bitter comedy of Bruegel, behind Velazquez is El Greco's tormented asceticism and ardent yearning for the transcendental. Just as Rembrandt reacted to the comic element without history, as he found it in Bruegel, by renewing the vision of history, so Velazquez reacted against his predecessor. In a century which saw the triumph of the doctrine of immanence, he practised, in the highest and fullest sense of the term, a painting of immanence. Velazquez was a humanist too, the supporter, even, of a new humanism; but, unlike Rembrandt, he made a thorough study of the ancients. He did not imitate them, however. When he took up a mythological subject—*The Triumph of Bacchus* (or *The Topers*), *Apollo at Vulcan's Forge*, *Minerva and Arachne*—he placed it in the present. But the present, for him, is a moment of lucid awareness, not of uncontrolled passion. In this he is opposed to Rubens, who had however a decisive influence on his development. He did not accept history as an eternal authority; nor did he reject it as a useless past; history for him delimits the sphere in which experience has completed and manifested itself in the consciousness, in the subject. His culture therefore is fundamentally critical; he countered Rubens with El Greco, in order to correct the sensualism of the first and the spiritualism of the second; he confronted the Carracci with Caravaggio (and even Poussin with Ribera); he combined the tonal painting of Titian and the lighting of Tintoretto with the coloring of Veronese. Francisco de Quevedo noted as early as 1629 that the harmony of his painting derived from the agreement at a distance of his patches of color, and that in this way he achieved the "truth," not only the "semblance," of feelings. In *Las Meninas* De Tolnay saw a statement of his poetics. The painter is at work among his models, within the picture space; his attitude, with the intent gaze, and the brush poised in his hand, is that of a man gauging a tonal value before attempting to fix its equivalent on the canvas; the space is purely pictorial, but it has a geometrical precision and clarity. The human consciousness has its own structure, which is in no way analogous with that of nature (even were one to recognize that nature has a structure). If painting is a total act of consciousness, the structure of the pictorial form is autonomous; it is in no way derived from an analogy with nature, not even from speech. Caravaggio, too, had repudiated speech and presented the image as an absolute reality. But Velazquez created a speech which could be uttered only through painting. If there is a message to be communicated, it does not consist in what is said or shown by the painting; painting can only communicate itself and, since it is an autonomous experience, clear and conscious, if it teaches something, it teaches that through the vision (and not only through philosophy or science) a clear, autonomous experience can be achieved, manifesting the artist's consciousness in its essence. Only in the late eighteenth century, when taste had become Neoclassical, did the *Triumph of Bacchus* appear to be a parody after the manner of Jordaens. To "demythicize" history Velazquez did not resort to the comic element. He was not like Caravaggio, a social rebel, nor like Rembrandt, a recluse; he lived at the Royal Court, where he was a Chamberlain and he carried out his duties meticulously. However, he kept his distance, preserved his independence and affirmed his human dignity. Velazquez is the first painter whose work may be said to reflect the doctrine of immanence (i.e. the conception of God as existing in and throughout the created world). He realized that the experience of painting is self-sufficient; it has no object beyond itself. As for man, it is in the sphere of conscious experience that he is truly himself, that he is free. To authority, Velazquez opposes neither revolt, nor indifference, nor resignation; but liberty, which is not evasion but self-awareness. So that while Rembrandt renewed and extended the content of painting, Velazquez created the structure of modern pictorial form; the first was the idol of the Romantics, the second of the Impressionists ("the painters' painter," Manet called him).

The third of the great humanists of the seventeenth century is Vermeer. He is also the one who comes closest to the spirit and thought of the Enlightenment. His picture of *The Painter in his Studio* has been described as a statement of his poetics: here the artist portrays himself, within the picture, turning his back on the world. In almost all his interiors the back wall is decorated with pictures, mirrors or tapestries, often shown on several successive planes. The picture is therefore the image of a picture, the fiction of a fiction. It takes its rise not as a representation of nature but of painting. In short, a painting cannot represent, cannot be, anything but itself. If Vermeer was no innovator of traditional Dutch themes, it is simply because painting cannot proceed from anything other than painting. It is a colored surface on which the colors create a certain space which can be measured, but which is "impracticable," like the space we see in a mirror. The problem of the mirror-picture, connected with the history of Flemish-Dutch painting since the time of Van Eyck, was certainly not unknown to Vermeer. But there is a difference between the mirror which receives the image and the human eye which perceives it. Pure optical perception may be likened to the reflection in a mirror, but actually it does not exist because the mind immediately takes possession of visual data and elaborates them. Our eyes see what our consciousness sees; thus perception gives us the structure and spatiality of consciousness. Painting is a conscious process of constructed perception. This intellectual process does not destroy perception in order to reach beyond it to an abstract concept; on the contrary, it intensifies perception, it constructs and gives it a spatial and existential framework. Vermeer is the only Dutch painter who can be said to give an intellectual representation of space, not merely an empirical or intuitive rendering of the surrounding world; but the intellectual process of constructing space is implicit in visual perception, which in itself involves a precise choice of values. The question of classical art, in which content or intellectual meaning is fully conveyed in the construction of form, is by no means eliminated. Vermeer resolves the problem by restating it in terms of the new perception-consciousness relationship, in a wholly modern manner, with the genius of a man who foresees the future, a greater innovator assuredly than those painters who held to "classical history" or "classical nature." Hence the fact that he was so soon forgotten after his death, and that his importance has only been appreciated in our time.

CLASSICISM

Classicism, in the seventeenth century, did not involve a blind acceptance of scholastic rules or a slavish imitation of forms inherited from the past. The most classical-minded of the seventeenth-century theorists, Bellori, felt the need to describe the artists of his time as "modern." Classicism was, however, chiefly characterized by its respect for the authority of history. It was a reaction against the Mannerism of the late sixteenth century in its two opposing and complementary aspects of "rule" and "caprice." It was a reaction, too, against the "realism" of Caravaggio and his followers, for "realism," in effect, sundered art from culture, denied the authority and even the experience of history, and reduced art to mere praxis. *If "rule" is rigidity, strictness, refusal to recognize experience, "realism" is disorder and tumultuous, uncontrolled experience. In equal opposition to these two extremes, classicism embraced the principle of order, not of rigid, hierarchical order, but of "natural" order. This was the view of the greatest classicist of the seventeenth century, Nicolas Poussin. "My temperament," he said, "forces me to seek out and love what is well ordered, to eschew confusion..." This love of order was so characteristic of Poussin that Bellori could write of him : " As he had read widely and observed much, no topic ever arose in conversation as to which he had not satisfied himself, and he marshalled his words and thoughts so readily and appropriately that it was plain that he had already considered the matter long and carefully."*

The order of things is determined by nature, the order of human affairs by history. The ideal condition, therefore, would be history enacted in a space and time which are "natural." Our notion of both nature and history is derived directly from the ancients; they acted in accordance with reason, and therefore with history, in a world conceived according to reason, and therefore according to nature. Having never known the Christian revelation, they had no experience of religious ecstasy; but they also knew nothing of the anguish and degradation of sin. And this was the dilemma—ecstasy and sin—which tormented the religious conscience of the seventeenth century.

NICOLAS POUSSIN (1594-1665). THE REALM OF FLORA, 1631. GEMÄLDEGALERIE, DRESDEN.

In the face of this dilemma classicism represented a principle of freedom. This is shown by the fact that the Carracci, whose aesthetic approach was basically classical, formulated an eclectic theory which allowed the artist freedom of choice. So classicism was, or purported to be, that true freedom which can spring only from man's experience of nature and history, in other words of culture.

In this sense, classicism was not the exclusive doctrine of the great seventeenth-century classicists, Annibale Carracci, Guido Reni, Domenichino, Poussin, Claude Lorrain and Le Brun; elements of classicism can also be discerned in Caravaggio, Rubens, Rembrandt and Velazquez.

For Rembrandt, classicism always remained a great repertory of images, even though he did not believe in the authority of classical history. A painting like the Rape of Ganymede undoubtedly has a touch of irony, even of satire. At any rate, by representing Ganymede as a mere babe abducted from its cradle, the painter wished to "de-mythicize" the theme and drain it of any allegorical meaning.

Rubens' intention was substantially the same in The Three Graces, a painting of three buxom Flemish women. He evidently wished to associate his own conception of beauty with a classical theme. His conception and composition were classical, but the subject was taken directly from life. In other words, the ideal structure of painting is always the same; but the forms in which it is expressed are manifold, and each period has its own.

REMBRANDT (1606-1669). THE RAPE OF GANYMEDE, 1635. GEMÄLDEGALERIE, DRESDEN.

PETER PAUL RUBENS (1577-1640). THE THREE GRACES, ABOUT 1639. PRADO, MADRID.

RHETORIC AND ARCHITECTURE

Rhetoric, as persuasive speech, is not necessarily bound to a literary text, nor must it be translatable in literary terms when it is employed in the figurative arts. For there is a rhetoric of architecture, just as there is a rhetoric of painting and of sculpture.

The architecture of the seventeenth century did not fundamentally renew the forms and types of classical architecture. It was content for the most part to develop the possibilities of variation for each type, and only rarely deviated from the original formal principle. It is an architecture of columns, pilasters, arches, friezes, etc., although the laws of proportion and symmetry, which determine the position and value of these elements in the design as a whole, are no longer respected. In architecture too, Mannerism had produced a break between the plastic form and its intellectual content. Defining the ideal conformation and proportions of the structural elements, it gave each of them a value in itself; it did not aspire to any other principle in their relation than rhythmical repetitions; it did not fit them into any pre-existing spatial structure; it gave them no other value than that of a simple image. An architectural iconography thus emerged, all the more free in its formal manifestations, because the space to which it related was no longer a hypothetical creation dependent on geometry and perspective, but a new urban structure.

Originally, each architectural element was the plastic form of a structural function; henceforth, as a result of the evolution of building technique, the structural function was independent of the equilibrium of the plastic values. But as these elements preserve the arrangement which they had when they were part of a system of forces and a spatial figuration, they become symbols of a function which no longer exists. The symbolic function thus replaces the real function; and the symbol no longer has an intellectual value, but a practical and communicational value. Architectural allegory developed throughout the century, and reached its height in the eighteenth century with the church of St Charles in Vienna, expressly designed by Sedlmayr from this point of view.

We have seen that façades are no longer the section of a perspective, nor the surface which closes off a building unit. As visual objects, they now belong rather to the street or the square than to the building of which they form part. Borromini went so far as to design façades whose axis deviates from that of the church, and which have no relationship with its interior. Seen along the length of the street, the church façade strikes a contrast with neighboring buildings; it holds out an invitation to enter. In this respect, its spatial or plastic quality is more marked than in the façades of civil architecture. It normally suggests two movements, one outwards, towards the street, the other inwards. The most typical example is the church of Santa Susanna (1603), designed by Maderna. The façade forms a decorative pattern built up around the keynote of the structure, the door. The engaged columns suggest a portico or pronaos, but one merged into the surface. The empty space of the door is magnified by the curving tympanum and the triangular pediment of the simulated portico; it is repeated higher up in the central window, and once again in the great pediment crowning the façade. In addition to these flattened projections, there are small, deeply recessed niches on either side containing statues. The frontal surface has thus been so much broken up that it almost ceases to exist. Its remaining planes serve as the connecting link between the architectural members which suggest an emerging plastic structure, and the recesses which suggest a receding perspective. Maderna was trained in the Mannerist tradition and tends to reduce the plastic to the linear. But Pietro da Cortona in Santa Maria della Pace, and Bernini in Sant'Andrea al Quirinale, make the entrance a veritable architectural organism, a columned portico, and develop this motif in the façade above the entrance. In the twin churches in the Piazza del Popolo, the classical form of the round temple, which Bernini himself had revived in working out the urban arrangements of the Pantheon, is reduced to the junction, on the same axis, of two essential elements: the portico, or entrance to the church, and the cupola, which symbolizes the heavens.

In the seventeenth century, the cupola too lost its function—established by Bramante in his design for St Peter's—as the crown of a well-balanced system of volumes. Michelangelo had tried to integrate it into the dynamics of the building as a whole, but in fact he removed it from the key position it had had in the static and plastic complex. Thus the cupola retained its original meaning as an allusion to the vault of heaven; but it could be raised or lowered, widened or narrowed, according to the play of masses in the building, and even according to the urban landscape around it. Henceforth the cupola of a church did not even have to correspond to the intersection of the nave and transept, nor did it necessarily occupy a central position in the ground plan. In churches with a central plan, it develops and compensates by its height for the perspective recession of the nave. In the church of Sant'Agnese, Borromini erected the cupola directly over the façade, so that the concavity of the latter is compensated by the convexity of the drum; and he raised it higher in order to oppose a vertical component to the longitudinal expanse of the Piazza Navona. Rainaldi, in Santa Maria in Campitelli, saw no need to build the cupola over the sacred area of the altar, and placed it in the most favorable visual position.

By being reduced to a purely representative function, the classical architectural elements acquired greater prominence, which explains why the structural members of Baroque architecture appear heavy, grandiose, turgid. They are designed to impress upon us the "monumentality" of the building, to display its ideological significance and allegorical content. The column, which is a static element of the monument, is a support whose shape, size and frequency are determined by the composite weight it has to bear. Since antiquity this static function had had its ideological equivalent; the column was an image of stability and strength. But now that the great problem of the Church was that of upholding its threatened dogmas, the column became a symbol of the stability of the faith. This symbolism is the more

obvious as there was often no longer any structural reason for using columns. In the colonnade in front of St Peter's, the enormous columns bear no weight; Bernini aligned them four by four, like figures in a procession. Perrault, in the façade of the Louvre, aligned the columns like a bodyguard of soldiers presenting arms. Rainaldi, in Santa Maria in Campitelli, hoisted them up to the second story of the façade like banners on flag-poles, repeating them like the hosannas of a hymn. Still more than symbols, they are emblems, or signs; but it would be a mistake to suppose that their function is only decorative. Columns, tympana, friezes, pilasters, and recesses preserve at bottom their original character as space-defining elements, and if they fail to achieve a spatial construction, they represent space visually, or rather they make an imaginary space visible. The great modeled friezes and the heavy cornices suggest a relationship between distant planes; the triangular tympana suggest the convergence in foreshortened perspective of two parallel vertical lines; the curved tympana recall the curvature of the horizon. One might almost suppose that this real architecture was designed in imitation of painted architecture; for its structure is not that of tectonic space, but of purely visual space. The architect's concern with visual effects drew his attention away from strictly structural requirements. Thus optical and psychological illusionism, both on the conscious and the unconscious level, became an essential feature of the building and was sought for its own sake. Artificial perspective, which pretended to give a true and exact representation of visual reality, and thus to determine the correspondence between the structural and plastic elements, no longer had any *raison d'être*, except as a special case within a much wider perspective framework. Bernini uses ordinary perspective, which projects the images on a curved rather than a flat surface. This is why he changed the original rectangular plan of St Peter's Square, making it first round, then elliptical; and accordingly corrected the perspective of the nave of St Peter's and of the Scala Regia. Guarini, in his perspective, took up the theory of projections, even going so far as to use cast shadows as formal and constructive values.

If the building no longer abides by the laws of construction in space, but makes space visible in the infinite variety of its possible forms, it is no longer a plastic form inserted into the perspective of space, but a crystallization of space itself. Dimensions become more important than proportions; more emphasis is laid on the contrast than on the harmony of verticals and horizontals; surfaces are developed endlessly, and planes multiplied; the relation between voids and masses is varied freely and rhythmically; allowance is made for chance plays of light; the plan is freely articulated, and the building is placed in close relationship with its natural setting. The common notion of space is no longer dictated by a mathematical principle, but by experience. Space is the city and the countryside, considered each for its own sake or in their relationship to one another.

This conception of the free relationship between the building and its surroundings rules out any distinction, in terms of value, between the external and the internal: the architectural space tends always to mark the limit of real space and the beginning of imaginary space. The first architect to realize this was Pietro da Cortona, in the church of Santi Luca e Martina. Space here is defined by the plastic articulation of the walls, and by the suggested projections and recesses in the surface of the architectural members. The function of the "plastic" wall is not unlike that of theatrical scenery; it defines at once the space in front and the unseen space behind. But because the spatial elements of this wall, projecting from it or receding into it, are not all equal, but on the contrary are variously modulated through an interplay of perspective foreshortenings, the wall cannot be taken in by the eye along a single line of sight; it can only be taken in by a moving spectator within the building. When the church has a central plan, as in the church of Santi Luca e Martina, and in most of the churches designed by Bernini, Borromini, and Rainaldi, the wall "unrolls" before us. The foreshortenings, projections, and recesses seem to develop or to contract under our very eyes; the columns rise up for a moment as if isolated, then take their place in the modulated surface of the wall. The consequence of this, which Rainaldi had already realized in Santa Maria in Campitelli, and which eventually led to the free designs of German Baroque churches in the eighteenth century, was the end of the traditional type of church, with either a longitudinal or a central plan or a combination of both. True, Fischer von Erlach and Balthasar Neumann (and also Vittone in Piedmont) revert to the dislocation of pillars in the interior, but only with a view to creating perspective vistas, "repoussoir" effects, and divergent or secondary perspectives.

archi.

The desire to display the divine authority and, of course, the political power of the state, and the prosperity of the ruling classes, is not sufficient to explain the grandiose demonstrativeness of Baroque architecture. What was the exact aim of this architectural rhetoric? What was it meant to demonstrate which could not have been demonstrated without architecture? We have seen that its great novelty was the idea that space does not enclose architecture, but is made visible through its forms; thus architecture presupposes nature, if only as the spatial setting of its elements. As forms became more complicated the naturalistic motif was increasingly developed until it predominated in the decoration; but it also hastened the break-up of the traditional building designs by introducing a freer movement of masses, a wider use of curving surfaces, and a closer connection of the building with its surroundings, whether park or garden, by means of flights of stairs, terraces, exedrae and projecting or receding building units.

Towards the end of the seventeenth century nature—water, trees, open sky—became an essential part of the urban setting. For Carlo Fontana the Tiber was the vital artery of Rome, just as St Peter's was the structural and historical nucleus of the city. His successors devised an "open architecture," with buildings and wings of buildings freely laid out and diversified with loggias, porticoes, stairways, terraces and parks dotted with pavilions and garden statues. Already in the early years of the century, moreover, Bernini had modified Maderna's designs for the Palazzo Barberini and made it almost a villa within the city. Architecture, in fact, had become a second nature grafted on the first and prolonging it with the help of the human imagination. Nature was the original setting of human life; architecture, whose highest form is the capital city, is the setting of civilized society. But there is a continuity between "natural" and "artificial" nature; man's handiwork does not contradict that of God but continues it, extends it, exalts it. In the frescoes of Gaulli and Pozzo, architecture towers into the heavens; it is the bond which unites the society of the living with the society of the elect. It is therefore a process of election. The art of *edifying* in the true and in the figurative sense of the word, architecture has the task of disposing the human mind to a life in one dimension, in a space without earthly limits. Being at once *elocutio* and *dispositio*, it has the dual aim of giving both pleasure and instruction.

4

THE FAÇADE

The most interesting problem of Baroque architecture is unquestionably that of the façade. Visually, the façade belongs to the external setting of the building, it forms part of the street or the square; it has a demonstrative function, a display value, in the public eye. But what it is designed to demonstrate or represent is the significance or import of the building to which it is connected. Generally, the façade is a complex organism, articulated and elastic, in which two opposing thrusts balance each other, one outwards, the other inwards. The urban space was thus no longer confined to that of the streets and squares; the internal space of a church, of a corridor or a courtyard, of the great staircase of a *palazzo*, is no less part of the urban complex for being closed off from the open street. It, too, is a place of social intercourse, for the life of the city goes on in this closed, interior space. The façade is therefore not a barrier, it is a partition; it does not close in or isolate, but connects; it enables communication. We may describe it as creating communication between two spatial entities, differing in scale and luminous intensity, but of equal urban and functional interest. Visually, this double thrust, outwards and inwards, is expressed in two ways, which are often combined: first, the alternation of projecting structural elements (columns, pilasters, tympana, cornices) containing niches and recesses which go to create perspective;

secondly, the inflection of the surface by means of contrasting curvature, now concave, now convex. Naturally, because the façade is, and substantially remains, a surface, these projecting and receding elements serve only as a form of denotation, not as plastic developments of the space. The spatial imagination of seventeenth-century man was no less sensitive to psychological stimuli than to visual evidence.

The evolution of the elastic façade, resulting from the double thrust inwards and outwards, can best be seen by comparing the façade of Carlo Maderna's church of Santa Susanna with the façade, much more inflected and sensitive in design, of Carlo Fontana's church of San Marcello; they date, respectively, to the first and last years of the seventeenth century. Or we may compare Bernini's façade for the Palazzo Barberini, in which the communication between external and internal space is entrusted to the great perspective openings, with Guarino Guarini's façade for the Palazzo Carignano in Turin, which is conceived as an immense elastic framework subjected to opposing tensions expressed in the contrasting curves of concave and convex surfaces.

Precisely because of its mediating function between internal and external space, the façade was not a scenic element but an organic part of the urban landscape; it tends to engage the urban space and to define it, not only as a layout or a condition of perspective, but as a plastic reality. It is due to the façade that the articulated mass of a monumental building becomes a nucleus in the urban network of streets and houses. Faced with the problem of adding a façade to St Peter's after he had transformed the central plan of the basilica by prolonging the east end of the nave, Carlo Maderna developed the façade lengthwise and limited its height so that it did not hide Michelangelo's cupola. The cupola, however, thereby lost its central position and passed into the background, almost to the horizon. Then Bernini, developing his colonnade as an open form, referred back to the closed volume of the cupola; that is, he took it as the keynote in the urban space of the square; but he also used Maderna's façade as a middle term, or pause, between the cupola and the oval of the square. Borromini, on the other hand, by hollowing out the façade of the church of Sant'Agnese in the Piazza Navona, brought the cupola to bear directly on the façade, thereby creating a vertical axis to compensate for the length of the horizontal axis of the Piazza. Here again, the façade serves as a connecting link between two opposed volumetric entities.

Pietro da Cortona, in Santa Maria della Pace, went as far as to destroy the unity of the façade, breaking it up into an assemblage of surfaces variously curved, distributed on different levels, and brought into harmony with the adjacent buildings and streets. Access to these was had by way of entrances put through the façade itself, as in the perspective vistas on the stage of Palladio's Teatro Olimpico at Vicenza. The curved portico itself, almost Bramantesque in design, is adjusted to the perspective axes of the streets leading to the church. The relation, too, between the façade and the interior is fundamental. In Baroque architecture, the façade is always in effect the cornice and development of the doorway to the church, and as such is an invitation to the faithful to enter; but we must not forget that the axis of the entrance leads directly to the high altar, and that this closes the perspective vista which meets the eye on entering. In the church of Sant'Andrea al Quirinale, Bernini emphasizes this perspectival and ideological relationship by separating the high altar from the body of the church by means of a monumental structure with coupled columns and a great pediment; this can be regarded as an "internal façade," which re-echoes the theme of the street façade.

THE FAÇADE

3

4

6

7

5

SANTA CROCE, LECCE   CHURRIGUERA

Baroque architecture had a special character of its own in Spain and, largely owing to Spanish influence, in the south of Italy. In spite of the feeble attempts of Juan de Herrera and the Italian G.B. Crescenzi to create something new, the severe Mannerism of the late sixteenth century continued for many years; innovations were confined, for the most part, to the excessive decoration of doorways and windows. Towards the end of the century, however, the "official" ornamentation of Mannerist architecture was swept away by the rise of the Churrigueresque style. The art of Churriguera originated in the decoration of retables, or altar screens, and gradually spread to the whole architectural structure; and as it contained many of the traditional motifs of Gothic and Plateresque ornamentation, it reintroduced these into seventeenth-century architecture.

Something very similar happened in southern Italy, notably at Lecce, where a local style developed which is best exemplified in the church of Santa Croce, begun by Francesco Zimbalo. The churches here were often old, of Romanesque or Gothic origin; the old structure was retained, while the decoration and façade were renewed in the style of the day. The prevailing taste now was for strongly projecting members (pilasters, columns, balconies, etc.), which had however no structural function; their chief purpose was to break up and animate surfaces, thereby accentuating the pictorial vivacity of the decorations and enriching the play of light among them.

The predominant influence in Latin American art is of course Spanish and Portuguese. No trace of local art, Aztec, Maya, or Inca, is to be found in architecture, whose forms were dictated by the religious or political authority of the conquerors. But the elaborate and colorful decoration of many churches reveals the persistence of the tastes, and sometimes the themes, of the native craftsmen. For political reasons it suited the conquerors to keep the local art traditions alive, or at least to modify them only gradually. But it is clear that these traditions were only those of a popular art, tolerated as a kind of folklore, in which very little survived of the great figurative art of pre-Columbian times.

FAÇADE OF THE CHURCH OF SANTA CROCE, LECCE (APULIA).

JOSÉ DE CHURRIGUERA (1665-1725). HIGH ALTAR OF THE CHURCH OF SAN ESTEBAN, SALAMANCA, 1693-1696.

CHAPEL OF ST CHRISTOPHER IN THE CHURCH OF LA COMPAÑÍA, BOGOTÁ, COLOMBIA.

The most important art center in the New World, and the one in which "colonial" art was most strongly affected by Spanish influence, was Mexico. The conquest was followed by an initial Plateresque phase; then came the period of the great cathedrals (Mexico City, Puebla, Guadalajara, etc.). Most of these churches were built on a longitudinal plan, with a transept, a cupola, and a nave subdivided by pillars; the dimensions were generally on a grand scale, and the interior was rich in paintings (usually canvases by local artists imitating Spanish prototypes in a provincial style), in gilded and colored carvings, and openwork screens enclosing an altar or a chapel. Often, as in the fortress-churches of the sixteenth century, the façades had flanking towers.

In the high South American plateau around Lake Titicaca, the ancient sacred land of the Incas, the tradition of native art continued longer than in Mexico. The churches were often built on the site of Indian temples, and their decoration was often inspired by themes from the native art of pre-Columbian times (Bolivia, Ecuador, Peru).

Brazil possessed its own Baroque style, in which Portuguese influence was naturally dominant. The Baroque of the great mining cities, particularly of Ouro Preto, has an original character of its own, which is lacking in the "Coastal Baroque" (at Recife for example), with its unbroken, luminous surfaces. The abundance of gold (its export was forbidden, to prevent aggravating the economic crisis in Europe), and a plentiful supply of rare woods and colored stones, were responsible for the rich decoration of Brazilian Baroque; indeed, the architectural structure was only a pretext for lavish ornament. The greatest South American sculptor of the time, Francisco Lisboa, known as O Aleijadinho ("The Little Cripple"), worked in the church of Sao Francisco at Ouro Preto; his bold and elegant carvings are strangely reminiscent of Late Gothic art in Germany.

THE CHURCH OF SANTA MARIA DEL ROSARIO, PUEBLA, MEXICO.

THE CHURCH OF SANTA MARIA DEL ROSARIO, PUEBLA, MEXICO.

TECHNIQUE

The limitless extension and dynamism of the "modern" world, the formation of complex social organisms like the state and the capital city, led inevitably to a renewal of the instruments of work and production. From this point of view, we may say that Baroque art is the great technical contribution to the Counter-Reformation, the Catholic solution to the concrete problem of human enterprise. If we agree with the principle of salvation by works, and concede the finalistic and soterial character of human action, technique must be "creative"; that is, it must continue in society the work of creation whose principle and pattern were laid down by God in nature. In so far as it is imagination, art is the natural way in which man may act; the more so because science, developing now on lines independent of religious dogma, and of philosophical speculation, worked out an applied technique which, being an epiphenomenon, cannot be strictly finalistic or soterial. The treatises of Ramelli (1588) and Zonca (1607) are proof of the possibilities offered, even in the practical field, by a scientific and no longer merely empirical approach to the problems of mechanics.

When in the last years of the sixteenth century, Domenico Fontana erected the obelisk in St Peter's Square and moved the Cappella del Presepio into Santa Maria Maggiore, he showed that an architect must also be an engineer who knows how to use techniques elaborated outside the artistic tradition and therefore possessing a purely instrumental character. But by adapting them to the purposes of art, he conferred on these techniques a finalistic meaning and value. The fact that Bernini and Pietro da Cortona separated the technique of construction from that of the visual or imaginative arts, shows that the former was already subordinated to the latter. In fact, the architecture of both of these artists, though visually perfect, is often defective as far as the constructional technique is concerned. This attitude was not a traditional one, but originated in the sixteenth century. On the social level, it sought to maintain the distinction between "mechanical" crafts and artistic activity, by placing the first at the service of the second. In fact only art considered as persuasive rhetoric is related to the higher activities of politics and religion, which deal with the spiritual salvation of humanity.

Borromini corrected the technical errors of Bernini by attaching a spiritual value to the *praxis* of architecture, and by emphasizing the inspired element that enters into technique (the *furor* of Leonardo, and later of Lomazzo)—an element already affirmed, in a revolutionary manner, by the painting of Caravaggio. If technique is not implied *a priori* in the natural world created by God, and is a purely human activity, the classical theory of art as mimesis collapses. Art is no longer a representation or parallel of nature, but the creation of a second, and different, kind of nature. Why set any limit to fantasy by separating it as a mere caprice from the "natural imagination"? Fantasy, too, is a product of the mind, and nothing authorizes us to believe that it works against the providential designs of God; it is neither abstract nor "chimerical," because its images, achieved by technique, are visible, concrete, real. They are added on, like a new series, to those of the created world, and do not repeat them. Modern man does not live in nature but in the city, and the city is a landscape designed and created by man. Its space is created by architecture; it is not a fictitious space, but an "other" space. It has other dimensions, other proportions, other rhythms; it does not repeat the equilibrium of nature (in which, in any case, no one believed any more), but has the impetus, the tension, the fury, the raptures, the rigors, the upsurges, and also the emptiness, of the human soul in its anxious yearning for the transcendental. Socially, human work finds itself promoted to the rank of spiritual activity. Bernini is a great master who conceives and directs; Borromini is a craftsman who creates on a sublime level. He climbs on the scaffolding, takes the trowel and chisel from the masons, changes the plan while executing it, creates image after image in an ever-increasing intoxication; feverish and unstable, his designs are not projects, but passionate attempts to master his materials. He unconsciously recreates the medieval workshop, the common effort of a group working towards a common goal. Bernini reproached him for this and accused him of being a "Gothic" artist. In this ascetic process, in this "edifying work," he enrols the whole "people." He despises noble materials, precious marbles; for him, everything can be done with brick and plaster, because value is not in the thing itself but in the workmanship. In his architecture, in fact, we see the finest workmanship of the seventeenth century; the product of a vast, harmonious, highly skilled brotherhood of stucco-workers, gilders, carvers and stone-cutters. Milizia criticizes him with his usual malice when he says that Borromini is more of a cabinet-maker than an architect.

The critical stage was reached in the work of Borromini's follower, Guarini, a Theatine monk, philosopher and mathematician. He was the theorist of calculated willfulness, who made his point by way of the absurd. Architecture for him is the work of fantasy, which consists in drawing up hypotheses. To verify a hypothesis does not mean to demonstrate it, but to put it into practice. To demonstrate it would mean to eliminate it as a hypothesis or a problem. Now, to eliminate the problematical element of human life is to eliminate God. Guarini carries Borromini's "extravagances" to a point where they become paradoxical, even paroxysmal. By multiplying the structural members, making them rise out of one another in an endless sequence, he abolished every principle of equilibrium in a giddy swirl of rhythms. But this extravagance obeys a superior form of reason; its rhythm implies an underlying mathematical principle. In Paris, Guarini made contact with the "occasionalist" philosophers. He believed that God is no longer revealed in motionless nature, but in the movement of thought and human activity. Every image conceived by the mind carries in itself the law of a transcendental rationalism, which is quite illogical. The technique of art gives visible form to thought; by the same token it manifests the presence of God in thought. And since the phenomenon which reveals God is

a miracle, technique appears as the means of producing a miracle. Guarini found in practical reason and technical reason the impulse which carried him to the level of transcendental reason.

The difficulty lay in the fact that if vision is always a phenomenon, every phenomenon tends to present itself as a vision; at the very moment when art strives to obtain its greatest effects, its most spectacular monumentality, it breaks up into an infinity of phenomena. Even a basket of fruit on a table, seen in a certain light, becomes a vision and a revelation. The artist has to turn everything into phenomena, he must visualize everything; thus technique is infinitely diversified. The techniques of vision are infinite: there are those of illusionism, of arrangement, of composition, of near and distant focusing. Infinite, too, are the techniques of execution; every artist has his *praxis*, and he often modifies technique according to the type of image. In painting, as in architecture and sculpture, the medium and the material are no longer concealed; the image has its own substance, and there is no reason for concealing it, for it is the material of nature. It is true that art should conceal art, but not in the sense of simulating nature. In painting, the texture of the pigments is often thick, heavy, unctuous; it retains the trace of the paint brush, of the artist's touch. To conceal art does not mean that what is painted must seem natural, it means to hide artifice, to make the observer feel that even the most complicated effects are obtained easily, naturally, at the first attempt. Fervent speech which is moving and pathetic is more persuasive than any other; without *furor* there can be no art; but just as speech must remain speech, so painting must remain painting. Here the gesture itself comes into play; the movement of the hand which applies the colors is as eloquent as that of the orator, and the rhythm of the colors on the canvas is as eloquent as the orator's gesture. Even the simulation of *furor* may be achieved in an inspired sweep of the brush, in a cascade of touches, which are perhaps not as demonstrative, but quite as persuasive, as a "flood of words." Such is the case with Maffei, whom Boschini admired especially for the disordered impetuosity of his pictorial language.

In the same way, following the example of Bernini, sculptors aimed at "naturalness" in rendering in marble the softness of hair, the warmth of the flesh, the shimmering folds of garments; they thus greatly extended the limits of an art which had hitherto been confined to a few "classical" types. Henceforth it was possible to represent in sculpture a wind-blown palm tree, a transparent dress, a waterfall. But always the aim was not the similarity of the sculpture with the natural object, but the naturalness of the image. One might even say that art referred back to nature only to show, by literal similarity, the naturalness of its own images.

Such was the concern now with the actual processes of artistic creation that sketches ceased to be, as in the past, rough drafts for the work of art. They were phases of inspiration, recorded moments which might or might not be used in the final work, but which retained an autonomous value, and indeed were often reproduced by engraving. Not all painters had recourse to preliminary sketches: Caravaggio, Rembrandt, and Velazquez worked out the picture as they went along, often changing it radically during the execution, or even recasting it altogether.

For painting, the moment of crisis occurred with the advent of specialization. Because the painter is a technician of vision, who must translate everything into visible forms, it was inevitable that categories of painters, or specialists, should be formed. Each "genre" had its own technicians, subdivided sometimes into secondary categories. Thus we find landscapists, portraitists, still life painters, and perspective painters; but landscapists were subdivided into "veduta" painters and painters of architecture and of ruins; and among still life

painters we find specialists in flowers, fruits, game, musical instruments, etc. They often collaborated in the same work, revealing thereby that the artists themselves believed there was a relationship between a certain category of objects and the technique suitable for representing them. The artist, being a technician of vision, is therefore one who reveals the value of visible things; this value emerges in the act and process of painting. It is for art to discover and define the value of experience, of life as it is lived. And since its scope embraces everything that is visible, everything that is possible, its sphere of action coincided with the social program of the Church, which was to show the necessity and the positive character of worldly experience as a stepping-stone to salvation.

In reaction against this grandiose technique of the image, and this cyclic relation between imagination and action, the artists of the following century sought to create objects rather than images—to do and act regardless of creative or spiritual values. This is the thesis of action for action's sake, of profit for profit's sake, of the limitless accumulation of riches to be reinvested in the productive process. This is the Protestant thesis in which Max Weber recognized the Calvinist basis of industrial production and capitalism. But this is evidently a class thesis, typically bourgeois, directed against the social and technical program of the Counter-Reformation, in other words against Baroque art, which in the last resort aimed at giving life to a technology more closely bound up with aesthetics than with science, and thereby creating, ultimately, a great "popular" art of universal appeal.

5

TECHNIQUE

In the first edition of Bellori's "Lives," the biography of Caravaggio is preceded by an allegorical image (an old woman) who, as the caption explains, represents *praxis*. The implication is that theory meant nothing to Caravaggio; all that mattered to him was the *praxis* of pictorial composition. The Mannerists opposed *praxis* to theory, as the practical aspect to the intellectual aspect of art; it was therefore considered as no more than a handicraft, and as such was despised. But now that theory had become less important and *praxis* had the upper hand, the manner in which he handled the paints was sufficient to characterize an artist. *Praxis* is technique, and if *praxis* does not confine itself to displaying or translating any given value, but realizes the value itself, we may say that technique is no longer manual execution but the process of determining values. In this sense, the seventeenth-century conception of artistic technique anticipated the modern view of technique as a productive and creative as well as an executive or repetitive activity.

Borromini was not a great constructor; for pure constructive invention, Bernini was far greater. But Borromini was a great *technician* of construction; for him, constructive invention did not precede the technical execution, but was developed and realized through it. Actually, in his case, we should not speak of invention, but of constructive inspiration.

If we closely examine a painting by Rubens we may have the impression that the technical execution is hasty and careless; this group of hands is evidently obtained with a few rapid, fluid brushstrokes. In fact, Rubens wished to achieve a light and color "value"; in order to *isolate* it, he eliminated all description of the object. Therein lay his prodigious technique. It is clear that this subordination of the painting to purely coloristic and luminous values could not have been preconceived; it resulted from the intensity and internal coherence of the painter's brushwork.

Among architects, no one gave more thought to the problem of technique as a generator of images than Guarini. The structural forms designed by him in the cupola of the Cappella della Sindone in Turin are a real *tour de force*; the beauty of the chapel springs from the rhythm which he develops beyond the limits of equilibrium, and from the perfect but precarious intersection of forces in tension. Even the perspective, hitherto only a formula for spatial construction, becomes a technique for creating images; theorists themselves consider it as a rule governing the rhythmic repetition and revolution of forms in space. It is true that technique is a product of rational thought; but human reason, which is God given, is itself a miracle and therefore capable of producing miracles. Thus it always surpasses itself; it progresses thanks to its own creative vitality.

"Technique and the Miracle," or "Technique and Providence," might serve as alternative titles for the *Miracle of St Philip Neri* painted by Pietro da Cortona on the ceiling of Santa Maria in Vallicella in Rome. The Virgin and angels invoked by the saint intervene to support the tottering scaffolding of a church under construction. The artist probably wished only to show a miracle; but he could not resist emphasizing the complicated structure of the scaffolding, as well as the physical or mechanical intervention of Divine Providence which guides a human undertaking, protects it, and corrects its inevitable mistakes.

If technique has any creative possibilities, it becomes a form of invention. The artist does not invent the image and translate it through technique; he invents a technique which produces the image. This explains why, in the seventeenth century, every artist worked out his own technique. This is not to say that he did not resort to imitation, because if *praxis* is not a purely mechanical process but a creative activity—the expression, that is, of a particular culture—it must inevitably have some foundation in nature and history. Imitation naturally presupposes an object; but this object does not remain purely external, immobile, and incidental. It takes on a new life in the memory and imagination of the artist, and is thus augmented by, or integrated with, a whole series of possible meanings which, when translated into visible reality, entirely transform its original aspect.

A good example of this is to be seen in Bernini's Fountain of the Rivers in the Piazza Navona where, with almost unheard-of boldness, he depicts a palm-tree bent and ruffled by the wind. The motive for his aesthetic excitement was, it need hardly be said, the beauty of this slender and flexible trunk, this wind-blown foliage bathed in light. But in the mind of the artist allusions and allegories were added to this theme; the palm-tree here refers to distant countries in which the rivers personified by the four figures flow; and to the old Christian symbol, of the faith spreading its life-giving shade into those distant regions of the earth. This revelation of an ideal meaning was inseparable from the technical feat by which the artist created trees, rocks, clouds and light for the first time in sculpture. Another technical prodigy was the luminous and graceful head of hair, the delicate filigree work in the bust of Louis XIV. This was no meticulous "copy" of real life; but these details define the space, as it were, in which the bust exists and help to bring it alive. The details assume a universal value, thanks to a technique which implies an individual conception of reality.

TECHNIQUE

1. Francesco Borromini: The Church of Sant'Ivo alla Sapienza, Rome, 1642-1650. Print from "Opera del Cavalier Francesco Borromini...," Rome, 1720.

2. Francesco Borromini: The Oratorio dei Filippini, Rome, 1637-1650. Print from "Opus architectonicum equitis...," Rome, 1725.

3. Guarino Guarini: The Cappella della Sindone, Turin. Print from "Architettura civile," Turin, 1737.

4. Guarino Guarini: Interior of the Dome, Cappella della Sindone, Turin, 1668.

5. Pietro da Cortona: Ceiling Fresco in the Nave of Santa Maria in Vallicella, Rome, 1664-1665.

6. Gian Lorenzo Bernini: The Fountain of the Rivers, detail, 1648-1651. Piazza Navona, Rome.

7. Gian Lorenzo Bernini: Bust of Francesco I d'Este, detail, 1650-1651. Galleria Estense, Modena.

8. Peter Paul Rubens: Sketch for the "Marriage of Marie de Medici," detail, 1622-1623. Private Collection, Paris.

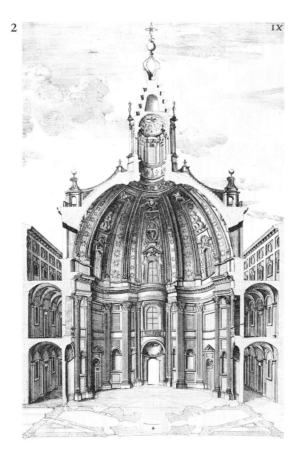

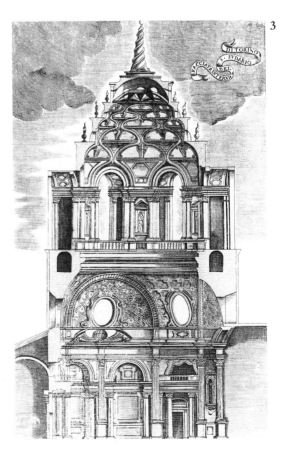

6

7

8

INDEX OF ARTISTS
LIST OF ILLUSTRATIONS

INDEX OF ARTISTS

LIST OF ILLUSTRATIONS

PHOTOGRAPHS BY

Alinari, Florence (pages 48 upper right, 72, 74, 106, 108, 109 above, 126), Anderson, Rome (page 73), De Antonis, Rome (pages 16, 36, 37), Archives photographiques, Paris (pages 49 above, 50 below), Maurice Babey, Basel (pages 13, 15, 26, 51, 56, 62, 63, 79, 83, 86, 89, 124, 127 upper left), Carlo Bevilacqua, Milan (pages 59, 82, 112, 127 upper right), Joachim Blauel, Munich (pages 96, 98), Lee Boltin, New York (pages 114, 116, 117), Bullaty-Lomeo, New York (page 58), Bulloz, Paris (pages 48 upper left, 50 above), Hans Hinz, Basel (page 99), A.F. Kersting, London (page 48 lower left), Raymond Laniepce, Paris (page 24), Louis Loose, Brussels (page 88), Studio Martin, Paris (page 49), Marzari, Schio, Italy (page 23), Portoghesi, Rome (pages 107, 125), Oscar Savio, Rome (page 109 below), Scala, Florence (pages 22, 60), Roger Viollet, Paris (pages 38, 48 lower right), Zoltan Wegner, London (pages 84, 85), of the Museo di Capodimonte, Naples (page 75), Museo Civico, Turin (page 37 below), and by courtesy of Ediciones Omega, Barcelona (page 127 below) and of the Oxford University Press (page 36 below).